SCM PRESS
PRESENTS

ἰδοὺ μυστήριον ὑμῖν λέγω
πάντες οὐ κοιμηθησόμεθα

I Cor. 15.51

A Bedside Book for RE Teachers

TERENCE COPLEY &
DONALD EASTON

SCM PRESS LTD

334 00094 7

First published 1975
by SCM Press Ltd, 56 Bloomsbury Street London

© SCM Press Ltd 1975

Type set by Gloucester Typesetting Co
and printed in Great Britain by
Fletcher & Sons Ltd, Norwich

CONTENTS

FOREWORD

H.M. Prison, Wormwood Scrubs

What a pleshah I ave to introdoos this tomb. I ave ad oppertoonity to read it over the larst foo yers and I can tell yer we wouldn't be wivvaht it dahn the scrubs. Even the screws as bin avin a chuckle. I bin arsked to write a foo woids abaht it for the public. I dunno why SCM don't arsk me to introdoos all their noo stuff, though praps they resoivin me for the best.

Whereas in their foist book they was on abaht the philosophy of RE nah they're on with ints on its apperlication. But this book aint only for RE teachers lookin for practical elp, it's for everybody interested – Further Education teachers, stoodents, parents, clergy and all interested umans – if yer lookin at this on some crummy bookstall and wonderin whether it's worth partin with yer money for yer can take my woid – this could be the edge against inflation we've all bin seekin. Mind yer, I wonder whether a 10% royalty is compensation for avin my name associated wiv these two shady characters, Copley and Easton. I arsk yer, is it really worth it?

Jake the Snake

BACKWORD

Here we are again. Welcome to the Bedside Book, guaranteed to produce insomnia among the backwoodsmen of RE. Welcome to RE for those to whom this has been a subject for slumber; RE the subject on the move! Bored and boring teachers must get off the roundabout before they get dizzy and sick and fall off; tub-thumping Christianizers can leave the classroom and buy a Do-it-Yourself home pulpit kit. This is the subject for the teacher interested in religious insights (from all religions), in non-religious stances for living such as humanism, even in anti-religious stances such as some brands of communism. He is interested in what makes people tick, in sharing with children his concern for the deep questions of life. He knows himself – where his own views and prejudices lie – and can come to terms with this so the classroom does not become a Christian or agnostic or humanist platform. For the teacher committed to this approach let him – as in the women's magazine serial – 'now read on'. The teacher who is less sure that this *is* RE would probably benefit from reading first our book *What they never told you about RE*.

Our aim in this book is to provide insights and help in some of the problem areas and perennials of secondary school RE. Part I is taken up with general guidance on matters of lesson-planning, the use of visual impact, narrative impact and discussion. Part II tackles problems that arise in all secondary RE: use of the Bible in the classroom and talking to children about God. Part III then tackles in detail some specific topics: miracles, life after death, the resurrection of Jesus, etc. Our criteria for selecting these is twofold: most appear on syllabuses for RE both ancient and modern as necessary topics for the growing child to consider, and most are frequently handled very badly. We didn't want to duck the question of moral education either, so we included one topic, advertising, as a very well-worn subject and another, friendship, as a subject so easily descending into waffle, platitudes and Victorian moralizing.

We wouldn't claim for any of this papal encyclical authority, but we have taught all these topics in the comprehensive classroom and are very well aware of all that the man on the shop floor of the job is facing. This is why, for instance, we have added a postscript on discipline, ignored by most books but essential to the success of any teaching.

Authors are fond of closing prefaces with pious hopes about the reader and what he may derive from the book. If we are allowed one lapse into pious expression it would be that our hopes for the reader are precisely those we have for the pupil in the RE lesson: first that he will thoroughly enjoy it and second that he may find it useful. What else can we say, except AMEN?

ACKNOWLEDGMENTS

No books nowadays fall from heaven, nor from the authors' pens without the help of other people. We are very grateful to John Bowden of SCM Press, especially for his willingness to be murdered in Chapter 14. SCM Press staff are claiming to have witnessed resurrection appearances, but some authorities suggest this is a tale put about by hysterical women (Luke 24.10f.).

Gill Copley was another accessory, whose helpful suggestions kept us in order for some of the writing of this text. We also thank Mrs Rita Luyke-Roskott for inside information on the Wizard of Oz, Mr Roy Stevens for suggestions on ME through literature, Mrs Kathleen Bawden who helped prepare the manuscript in its early stages and Miss Glenis Copley who prepared the final typescript, all at risk of assassination by rival organizations. Finally, those with a delicate ear may catch the Scrubs WI Choir singing a plainsong setting of the Grieg Piano Concerto in the Appendix.

CHAPTER ONE

In Which Pooh finds the Grand Plan

OOH WAS COUNTING HIS POTS OF honey after breakfast when there was a knock at the door and in came Rabbit.

'Now come along, come along,' said Rabbit importantly, 'and you'll be in time.'

'In time for what?' said Pooh.

'You won't be in time for anything if you don't hurry up,' said Rabbit. So they set off. But on the way they met Piglet, who was looking for haycorns, which seemed as good a thing as any to look for.

'Hello, Piglet,' said Pooh, 'we're in a hurry.'

'Can I come too?' said Piglet, 'It's fun to be in a hurry.'

'We're not hurrying very fast while we stand talking here,' said Rabbit.

'Well I think I prefer hurrying slowly,' said Pooh, who was a bear of Very Little Brain.

'Do come on,' said Rabbit impatiently, so they all set off.

'Where are we going, Pooh?' said Piglet.

'Where are we going, Rabbit?' said Pooh.

'Well,' said Rabbit as importantly as he could while still hurrying, 'we're going to school.'

'Oh,' said Pooh.

'Ah,' said Piglet.

'So,' said Rabbit, 'we must get there on time.' They trotted on through the forest and started to jog down by the side of the stream. After a bit Piglet said,

'Pooh, what's a school?'

'Well,' said Pooh, 'it's a place-where-you- learn-things.'

'What sort of things?'

'Oh, just things.'

'Oh.'

There didn't seem to be any more to say. So Pooh hummed a little song to himself.

> I'm going to school, tra la, tra la,
> Although I'm no fool, tra la, tra la,
> I'm going today, hurrah, hurrah,
> And I'm on my way, hurrah, hurrah.

Soon they came to a sign:

SKUL

'Here we are,' said Rabbit.

'Here we are,' shouted Piglet excitedly.

'Here we are,' said a low, gloomy voice, 'here we are and nothing's happened yet.' It was Eeyore.

'Don't be impatient,' said Rabbit impatiently, 'the lesson's going to start soon.'

'Whenever I go to things,' said Eeyore, 'they start late. There's no consideration of others, that's what I say.'

'This is a place-where-you-learn-things,' said Piglet proudly. Pooh thought he'd like to learn how to get more honey and how to fit extra meals in to eat it and how to do lots of things and remember things he'd forgotten, but the teacher arrived. It was Wol. Wol coughed in a quietening sort of way so they quietened down and waited.

'Now,' said Wol, 'this is a lesson. It's about religious education.' Pooh wondered if you could eat it, but while he was wondering Wol showed them a Visshualade. It was a bright piece of paper with

RILIDIS EDICASHON

on.

'Wol, you are clever,' said Piglet. Wol coughed in a sort of satisfied way.

There was a pause.

'Have we finished now?' asked Eeyore wearily, 'because I've a lot of jobs to do.'

'Of course not,' said Rabbit crossly, 'let him carry on.'

Wol didn't seem keen to say more, but he did try a little harder.

'Well, this lesson is about religious education,' he said.

'He's said that already,' said Eeyore.

'This is exciting,' cried Piglet, 'I've never seen a lesson before.'

Pooh nodded sleepily.

'Well, you don't exactly see a lesson,' said Wol.

'Can you eat it then?' asked Piglet.

Pooh perked up.

'No.'

Pooh perked down.

'No, a lesson is sort of invisible,' Wol continued, 'you know when it's finished because, well, because it's over.' But Pooh was sliding into dreamland. It was a Rather Confused Dream. In it Christopher Robin was waving a piece of paper marked Grand Plan for Lessons, and there were lots and lots of hints in it for teachers and Pooh couldn't remember many of them because bears aren't teachers and nobody expects them to remember much. But Christopher Robin was reading some aloud.

'All lessons should have clear aims, otherwise the class can't follow what they're about. The test of this is whether an observer at the back of the classroom could write down the aim at the end of the lesson. . . .

'All lessons must have a very lively start, otherwise bears of Very Little Brain will fall asleep. A lesson can be won or lost in the first five minutes, and for student teachers this could be as little as two or three minutes. . . .

'All lessons must be carefully prepared, otherwise the whole impression given is one of not caring, and this spreads to the class; experienced teachers mustn't use experience as an excuse not to plan and think over carefully lessons on a topic they might have taught for years. . . .

'All lessons should change pace and activity, question and answer, writing, reading, discussion, to keep the class interested, and it is particularly important that double periods are not simply used as extended singles, with longer talking followed by longer writing—the pace must vary more. . . .

'When setting homework for bouncy people like Tigger the work set should be planned in advance so as to supplement usefully what has been done in class and not appear a spur of the moment torture; creative homework, with if possible a choice of topics, is desirable, rather than just routine chores. . . .'

Pooh thought all this was a very far cry from honey, but Christopher Robin continued.

'All lessons should start within the experience of the class and relate to them. For bears this would be honey, but the lesson would go on to widen their experience.'

'Hmmm,' thought Pooh, who wasn't too sure that he wanted his experience widened.

'Also,' said Christopher Robin, 'the lesson should have a good re-cap, written or oral, to get the point over. This provides the base for the start of the next lesson. . . .'

'Then there's classroom polity, that must be planned too. Come and look at this.'

In the dream he took Pooh into a large room in which were Rabbit's relations, all the younger ones, all sorts of shapes and sizes, all running round and shouting, while at the front, beaming in a sort of vacant way, was Kanga.

'This,' said Christopher Robin, 'is a group work lesson gone wrong. You see she hasn't helped them to see the aim of it, or planned it in such a way that they can all be busy while she helps those with difficulties. It's a great mistake to think that noise is always healthy.' He looked pained as two young mice ran over his feet.

'And in this sort of atmosphere,' he continued, 'it's hard to spot the real problems. Look over there.' In a corner sat a hedgehog who had obviously been waiting for help for a long time. He was looking prickly.

'He's wasted half the lesson waiting to get attention,' said Christopher Robin.

'But does this happen in real schools?' asked Pooh.

'I think so,' said Christopher Robin, 'the trouble with grown-ups is that they make all sorts of rules like those in my Grand Plan and then forget them when they get into the classroom. To do this sort of group work means that they ought to have lots of suitable material for the children to use.' He ducked as an exercise book flew overhead. 'And you need a good "lead lesson" to interest them. And most of all you've got to be in control just as much as in more formal lessons.' Pooh was more interested in watching a fight that was developing in one corner between a crow and a rook (he wasn't sure which was which) over a work-card, which tore. In another corner two fashion-conscious peacocks were talking about the latest in feathers; a pug puppy was whistling pugnaciously above the other babble.

'What bad children,' said Kanga. Nobody heard.

'I shan't tell you again,' she said. Nobody listened.

'We shan't have our lovely story if you don't quieten down.' The noise level gave no hint that they were remotely interested in having their lovely story.

'I don't think I want to see any more,' said Pooh.

'Come in here, then,' said Christopher Robin, and in the dream Pooh was in another room, with rows and rows of desks of silent young animals copying notes from the blackboard, supervised by a ferocious eagle, who glared at every loud breath.

'This is formality gone wrong,' said Christopher Robin. Pooh nodded. He hadn't the faintest idea what formality was, but he preferred the quiet lesson.

'You can see they're working harder,' Christopher Robin whispered in case the eagle heard them, 'but they haven't been given the chance to create or think. They're just listening and copying.'

'Couldn't you somehow mix the best of both these lessons?' asked Pooh.

'Well, classes like a variety of types of lesson, and each of these types can work, with very careful planning. But the teacher really plays a vital part in both. He's got to interest them, help them to think, and sometimes *make* them work.' A bell rang. They found themselves in the corridor.

'Is the school on fire?' asked Pooh.

'No, it's dinner time.' said Christopher Robin. At this point a rumbling they had been aware of for a while began to get louder and louder and nearer and nearer. Finally it became so loud that they couldn't talk any more. Suddenly round a bend in the corridor they saw it, ears flapping, head down, charging pell mell towards the dining room – a Heffalump! A Heffalump in full flight!

'Oh,' cried Pooh joyfully, 'a Heffalump! a Heffalump!' But a voice was waking him. . . .

'Pooh, Pooh,' called Rabbit, 'wake up, the lesson's over. We're going. home.'

'What did Wol say?' said Pooh.

'Well,' said Piglet, 'he said it was over.'

So Pooh sang another song.

> The lesson is ended
> Which Wol made a mess of
> And less of the lesson

And more of it mended
Would be quite effective
But lots of invective
And teacher as preacher
Has got a dim future.

'That doesn't rhyme properly,' said Eeyore bitterly.

'Never mind,' said Pooh, 'you can come in and share my honey with the rest of us.' Even Eeyore brightened up at this thought and as they went in Pooh said,

'I've had a Rather Confused Dream,' and he told them all about it.

'You know,' he ended, 'I don't think I'd enjoy being a teacher as much as I enjoy being Pooh, but if I was a teacher I think I'd need to remember the Grand Plan for preparing my lessons.'

'I bet real teachers don't remember it,' said Eeyore prophetically. But Pooh was too busy with the honey to talk any more.

CHAPTER TWO

The Quest for the Holy Nail

ONG YEARS DID THE COMPANY OF the Round Table travel in search of adventure in chivalry's name. Fill many a book their noble deeds could well. Yet erstwhile lay one quest more, the more challenging since unsolved, the Quest for the Holy Nail. Not since the Black Knights rode out from the land of Bim would the Company be so tried, yet lacking found. Scarce even with the wisdom of Merlin would they succeed in this endeavour. It came to pass thuswise.

In the fifth year after Sir Tupton's mark, when his son Sugbad still rode as his esquire, King Arthur summoned the Company and said,

'How say you to this? The Holy Nail hath vanished. Not since it came from Philistia's shore have such sad events o'ertaken it. Yet to us is given the power to remedy this, if ye consent to take up arms and try the tryst anew.' Their lined faces and white hair showed the years of toil, but wisdom linked with valour shone.

'Will ye try?' quoth their king.

'Aye, we will, for God, King Arthur and the Nail!' they cried, and held heads high. The Council ended, but with Merlin's wise advice.

'Discussion profits little, unless conclusion's reached. Then those involved can feel their part worthwhile. Else in parting they lose heart, and feel that talk hath led to nought, no advance on ere the session started. But if conclusion's found, discussion then is crowned. Give heed to this.'

Each man went to his horse, and then rode out to scour the land.

North rode Sir Guthlac until coming hard by an inn halted for a while. He purposed by skilful discussion to enquire what the peasantry knew in the matter of the vanished Nail.

'I heard tell of a Nail,' quoth he, and waited for response. None came. And here was wise Merlin's absence sorely felt. For truly could not Guthlac hope to hear a good response, ere yet he'd made them party to the facts.

'Hast *thou* heard of the Nail?' he said to an aged man.

'Aye,' replied the ancient, 'I have heard of many a nail.'

Sir Guthlac waited breathless.

'What be thou,' he said at last, 'canst thou help me in the matter of the Nail?'

'I can nail thee sure,' rejoined the peasant, 'for I be undertaker to this town.' The others roared with laughter.

'Thou canst ask those with no ideas to talk with no information to aid them,' said the innkeeper, 'but thy discussion will be barren.'

So ended Sir Guthlac's quest in derision.

Sir Vere fell not into that snare. He rode south and swift, and coming at even to a village gave to the peasants each a parchment, setting out the Nail, its history (with pictures) and enlisting their support in the Quest, with questions. A better start had he than Guthlac. So at outset his discussion fared much better, for informed it was and better answers had he. But to no purpose, for he heeded not a jot. Truth to tell, i'faith, he heeded not because he thought he knew the answer and listened only to steer his peasants to that end, so missing their clues, and angering them by ignoring their sincere opinions. At last they dealt with him roughly and refused to say more. He took leave in umbrage, and on the wrong road.

Alas, Sir Pugliff came to grief more quickly. He enquired for help among the peasants of the east. But two spoke out and drowned their fellows' words (and thoughts). These two varlets had but one aim, to wreck his discussion by loud-mouthed stupidity, and by shouting down all else. Sir Pugliff took them too seriously, and having not the sense to control his discussion could make no headway. He may be at the same place still.

Sir Cumference rode round the whole area, but never reached the point, so his quest and discussion ended in an eternal circle of vagueness.

Sir Mon, for giving exhortation out of place, was quickly finished by the peasantry.

At times the errant knight Sir Cumstances helped the Quest. At others hindered he their labour. For oft he could control the peasantry, affecting how they helped by extremes of weather, ventilation, crowded rooms to hold the converse in. A knight to watch, this Sir Cumstances, and if possible to enlist in the Quest.

Sir Lancelot rode west and he at length brought the Quest to its conclusion and a clear ending it had. He sensed the situation. He bethought himself whether it might be right in groups to put the peasants, in each appoint a chairman to control (the rowdiest peasant oft best chairman makes, in quietening others silences thus himself) and designate recorders to write down the agreed conclusions of each group and make report to full council. Each peasant would be then involved much more than in full session.

Then pondered he if it might be right to handle the questioning himself. Groups or full session might work well at different times, but Lancelot wisely chose the latter course, not knowing these peasants well, reasoning thus that he could check thereby their talk and if perchance it wandered from the point could return it thither. If he had known them well he might have ta'en the other part, but he chose wisely in this for, though each member contributed less than if in a small group to boot, Lancelot could pick with skill the main points of their talk (which else he might not hear) and supplement his questions well, e'en though the aim be open.

Nor hogged he all the talking for himself as some chairmen are wont to do (methinks they fear a silence else they long to check the working of their vocal chords). So started he his discussion with an open end in view – no solution to the Quest sought he by force or guile to impose. But how to keep th' attention of the peasantry? He perceived well the difficulties he must traverse. For how should peasants stay alert through the long vigil for the Holy Nail? Truly he perceived that no peasant would list for long, nor heed with careful thought were his discussion lightly ta'en. Considering the which he made them do preparatory and follow-up scroll work in the library. He made them write some answers and mixed the talk with what they called real work. He showed them the importance of the question they discussed and what it meant for them (if the Nail were not found the monastery would close and Sir Abbot could not buy their produce). He listened sympathetically to each man's opinion, not taking side, nor appearing to despise any, sometimes asking further question shrewdly to draw the silent members in, if but a 'Yea' or 'Nay' and thus to give them confidence. The ridicule by some of sincere views of other peasants crushed he.

Yet even so as time went by Sir Lancelot saw that dullards yet among the peasantry had little grasped of what had passed. And yearned he sore that they should understand and contribution make. At length he thought and hard, the session o'er, as how he might progress when morning came. At last his furrowed brow eased into fallow for a time: let them play the roles themselves and act the parts to make the abstract real. Then they would understand if – inhibitions gone – they'd join the act. What sport but jousting else could compete for interest with improvisation to help them see the point? So he made progress further.

Not only that, he used a visiting knight, Sir Gad, to help the question on: not to lecture to the peasants, which might bore, but just to answer questions as on trial, thus to expound his views. This outside speaker, used in moderation, helped discussion on, as did the high regard in which Sir Lancelot held his friend, Sir Socrates. Sir Socrates would always throw the question back provoking more his questioners than if he put himself on trial and defended his position. So when one said, 'Do you believe the Nail exists?', Sir Lancelot answered, as Sir Socrates had shown, 'What dost thou mean by Nail? What image of it hast thou in thy mind?' By these and other means he questioned them at length and probed their thoughts and made them think more deep. At last he summarized for them the progress they had made, so that they saw that the talk had served some purpose.

The Nail must surely by the Shrine of Blessed Ponsford be,
Where aged pilgrims and the faithful young ones bow the knee;
'Tis there will be solution to this mystery;
But thou, O RE teacher, canst thou truly see
That thy discussion will be Purgat'ry
Unless it heeds the hints we've given thee?

CHAPTER THREE

Goldilocks and the
Three Bears

ONCE UPON A TIME THERE WAS A little girl called Goldilocks. She lived in a little house with her mummilocks and daddilocks on the edge of a big forest. Goldilocks loved to wander in the forest to pick the pretty flowers and to hear the sweet birds sing. One day as usual she was doing this, but she wandered on and wandered on and wandered on until at last she was far from home. But there in front of her stood the most beautiful little cottage, with sweet-scented flowers in the garden. It looked so inviting that Goldilocks decided that, since no one seemed to be at home, she would just peep inside. Just a peep, she thought, and went in.

But as soon as she was inside she could smell a smell. Her favourite smell. Porridge! And there on the table were three bowls of porridge: a big one, a medium one and a little one. How tempting it looked! So going to the big bowl she picked up the spoon. Just a spoonful, she thought, and popped it in her mouth. But the porridge was far too hot and she burnt her mouth. Try the next bowl. She did, but it was too cold. But the little bowl? Just right, and she gobbled it all up. Now when she had eaten the porridge she noticed three chairs: a big chair, a medium chair and a little chair. So she fancied a sit down. Just for a minute, she thought, and sat on the big chair. Too hard. She tried the medium chair. Too many cushions. But the little chair was just right, and so she sat on that. Until suddenly—crash! It fell to pieces under her weight. So she ran upstairs and there were three beds: a big bed, a medium bed and a little bed. Of course she tried the big bed. Too big. And the medium bed. Too big. And the little bed – perfect. She fell fast asleep.

But soon the owners of the cottage returned, three bears: Daddy Bear, Mummy Bear and little Baby Bear. They saw the empty porridge bowls and the broken chair and Daddy Bear said:

'Okay, youse guys, it's time dis crummy story gotten pepped up. De lousy boring presentation's fine for dullsters, but it sure is boring as pizza on a wet night.' He looked at the porridge bowls.

'Some dame's spoofed 'em up,' he went on, 'looks like her fat frame busted up your chair, junior.'

'Gee, Pa,' said Junior, 'that's real mean. We bin exploited again in some ham story.'

'Yeah,' said Ma, 'I bet she's messing the beds upstairs. I sure am tired o' this tedious routine.' She spat her gum out.

'What say we tell the woild how to tell stories good an' settem right?' said Pa.

'Sure,' said Ma.

'And I'll get the cops to put an APB on Goldilocks,' said Junior, 'the way this story's told she always freaks off and leaves us to get another goddam chair from Schreiber.' He went off to the phone.

'Okay, woild,' said Pa, 'this is how to make out real good in the story-tellin' line. It's sure useful to be able to spin a good yarn. Ya gotta remember, everybody loves a story and them as is too old for a story is too old. It's the oldest teaching aid in existence and the kids sure love it like they love popcorn.

'Now some bums'll tell ya ya gotta be a born story-teller. There aint no sich thing. You guys gotta watch good story-tellers at woik and see how they do it; why, aint bin a baby born tellin' stories, so don't fall for the hoodlum's talk about born story-tellers. Throw away ya inhibitions and have a go. Why, we bin moidered by story-tellers so many times afore in this Goldilocks saga that we can take a few more knocks from stoodents tryinalearn.

'When ya gotta story ya gotta get structure. Ya gotta make it woik towards the theme ya using it fo'. Take our story, frinstance, ya could use it to illustrate several themes – notta go into a strange house, or always ta keep a guest bed handy, or notta get lifts from strange bears. Get it straight, you guys, ya story's amorphous till it's bin structured.

When ya gotta thread runnin' through, git the thread in ya head so it comes out in the tellin'. That's de foist thing.

'Then ya gotta have empathy with the characters. Aint no use presenting the Pharisees as wicked bears that was outa slam Jesus. They wuz real yuman guys, with yuman intentions, trying to obsoive a law an' intoipret it frevery situation. There's their side o' the argument. Ya gotta feel for all the characters in ya story.' He paused, polished his dark glasses and then lit a cigar.

'Now you guys gotta stop bein' stoopid boring joiks. The Nine o' Clock Noos voice is okay fo' the Nine o' Clock Noos mebbe, but not fo' story-tellin'. Ya gotta vary tone, pace and face (don't look like a plank from the morgue), use pause an' other little knacks. Use ya licence, story-tellers' licence (the cops sell em cheap) – the kids sure sense when ya not bein' literal, like if ya talk about Nero's E-type chariot or about the pharaoh seein' on telly how the Hebrews wuz expandin'. Ya can be honest and tellem when legend creeps in – they mustn't assoom that they've gotta be literal.

'The key woid is re-enactment, not narrative. Narrative's flat, ya can read it (if ya can read). Re-enactment is 3D stuff. De good storyman re-enacts the story. Practise it in front o' ya dressing table mirror or ya gal. My woman's seen me do more faces than the Arabian Nights; they wuz pretty square.

'Now ya gonna say, does it always have to be me, jazzing all the parts? Hell, no, ya can frinstance get the kids to dress up and mime the parts as ya tell it (living viz. aids) or ya can build ya story around several pictures if ya want. But be young again, you guys, let it thrill ya.

'Some smart creep soon gonna say "How ya keep de little guys in order while ya tellem de stuff?" I'll tell ya, ya lousy creep. Ya don't need shooters or boxing gloves or gang support. If ya planned it careful and practised it, if ya keep the action moving, if ya entertain and use yumour, if ya pause from time to time to question 'em, the story'll keep 'em in poifect order – it'll grippem better'n handcuffs. The discipline problem's a non-starter in this.' He paused to throw away his cigar stub.

'I gotta go now to help Ma straighten out that broad upstairs. But remember, you guys, stories is de greatest teaching gimmick in de woild. But ya gotta use 'em good.'

Grinding his cigar stub into the floor and reaching down a nearby meat-cleaver, Daddy Bear turned and began to stomp upstairs.

CHAPTER FOUR

Off to See the Wizard

WHAT A WIND IT WAS. IT BLEW AND it blew and it blew. Dorothy paced the front of the room waiting for her class to arrive. They were very late; break had ended five minutes ago. That was the trouble with transportable classrooms – children took so long getting there.

She began to tidy up the pens and ink and books and chalk. *What* a wind! It was a good thing Aunt Em had put the washing out a day early.

Then all of a sudden it happened. The wind gave a great shriek, the classroom lurched off its frame, whirled round, and soared up and away into the air.

They clattered into a musty waiting room. Concrete floor, leather benches, barred windows, burnt-out grate. Dorothy opened a magazine and quickly closed it again. She sat down. Out of the corner of her eye she stole a glance at her companions. Strange how, ever since she had come to ground in this land so far from home, so many others had joined her on her journey to the Sapphire City to petition the Wizard himself, the Great and Terrible.

'Just look at us!' she thought. 'A head teacher with no head, a writer with no sanity, a book with no Part II, a bed with no sleeper. Even the classroom furniture positively insisted on coming; and here it all is: a room with no pupils, a board with no pictures, in short a lesson with no interest. And me in my gingham dress and pretty pink bonnet. What *would* Aunt Em and Uncle Harry say if they could see me now?'

Footsteps sounded in the corridor outside, and the door was flung open.

'Dorothy Gurgenfeld, come with us!' barked a voice. A hand grabbed her collar and hurtled her through the door, along the corridor, downstairs, upstairs, round the corner, down a corridor, through a door, and on to the floor. The door clanged shut.

She lay in a tall, vaulted chamber with gleaming pillars which swept up to a sparkling ceiling. In the wall in front of her stood a softly-lit door, and over it a beautiful sapphire lamp. Somewhere a mouth-organ played a lilting, haunting melody.

'This must be the Wizard's audience chamber,' she thought. 'I do hope he won't really be very terrible.'

The door under the lamp swung silently open, and behind it she saw a strange sight. On a glistening throne there rested a huge, pasty-faced head in a blue helmet with silver star on the front. From either side of the throne, from a drawing pin, hung an arm, while under it stood a huge pair of black boots.

The boots arched themselves and rolled from heel to toe and back again. The right hand swung up to touch the peak of the helmet. The head rolled its eyes and opened its parchment mouth.

'Evenin' all,' rasped the voice. 'I am Fuzz, the Great and Terrible, otherwise known as Dixon of Dock Green. Y'know, it's a funny thing but you never can get children interested if your lesson has no impact. And one of the best ways of making an impact is by illustrations.

'Now take young Dorothy. Came wandering into the Sapphire City the other day worried no end. She'd lost her pupils, got no illustrations, no impact, and she was really down in the dumps. Well, we soon managed to straighten things out. I took her on one side and gave her a bit of advice. "Evenin' all," I said, "Y'know, it's a funny thing but you never can get children interested unless you take them on one side and say, 'Evenin' all, Y'know, it's a funny thing, but you never can get an interesting lesson if you don't go to your teacher and say, "Evenin' all. Y'know, it's a funny thing but . . ." ' " . . . .'

'This is ridiculous,' shouted Dorothy. 'I've come all the way to the Sapphire City to get your help, and all you can do is sit there and say "Evenin' all." '

'Evenin' all,' said the head defiantly.

'Shut up.'

'Evenin' all,' it muttered.

'If you say that once more I'll knock you right off that silly throne.'

A tear of rage welled up in Fuzz's eye and trickled down the putty cheek. One of the boots stamped itself, but Fuzz kept his mouth tightly shut.

'Now perhaps you'll tell me how to get my pupils back.'

'Illustrations,' grunted Fuzz.

'What do you mean, illustrations?'

'What I say; illustrations. Use them.'

'Why?'

'Because they add so much to your lesson: colour, variety, humour, inspiration. In short, they give it impact.'

'Good. Now we're getting somewhere. But I still don't understand when to use them.'

'Any time. To start the lesson – that way you capture the interest immediately; or as you tell a story; or at the end when pupils are working on their own pictures. You can even make a whole lesson of it to sum up a lesson-series. In that case it's a good idea to discuss its structure and content first; and perhaps a diagram would be more suitable than a picture. I can show you several ways of organizing diagrams.' Fuzz paused to rub his silver badge. With a hiss and a sound of ringing glass the air was suddenly filled with diagrams. Dorothy whisked out her standard issue CIA/KGB Spymatic camera to take some quick shots. But by the time the diagrams faded she had been so busy that she had scarcely noticed them herself, so she had to think of something polite to say.

'I thought they were very nice,' she said.

'That's because they were well planned.' Fuzz looked a little smug. 'I'd thought them all out before you arrived – structures, colours, postures, expressions, dialogue – the lot. And that includes clothes, labels and captions to show who's who in the pictures, and to bring out the point of the lesson; even one or two of the jokes, too. Exaggerations and anachronisms always go down well. You should follow my example: plan in advance. Make your pictures good enough to inspire but simple enough not to deter.'

'You seem to be very keen on visual aids.'

'Not to the point of obsession. Remember, they are only aids. They're not a substitute for good teaching and they're not the only way to make a lesson interesting. And they are not just there to be copied. They are there to excite and provoke, and to fix the lesson in your pupils' minds. But they're not enough on their own. Use them together with notes or questions or hints. You've got to think of the whole child.'

'And what about film-strips and slides?' asked Dorothy. 'Do they help?'

'Not often,' answered Fuzz. 'They're over-rated. Part of the trouble is that there are so few decent film-strips in RE. Most are scenes of life in Bible-times, or pictorial sermons. And in the age of colour TV, so many appear poorly produced. Then there are the practical difficulties; you don't want to give a lecture but it's not easy asking questions in a darkened room. It's probably best to show only a few slides at a time; if we refuse to plod through a whole text-book, why are we still so pleased to plod through a whole filmstrip? A useful tip is to cut the filmstrip into slides, and to show these individually. One or two slides may well be worth showing, although you have to weigh this against the time it takes to put up the projector and mess around with the blinds.

'I think board-work has the advantage most of the time,' added Fuzz. 'Children can see a picture taking shape in front of them. It's an event, it's something vital in an age of mass-produced visual aids with which many teachers bore their classes. It helps to mark off RE as a subject which is dynamic and original.'

'I see,' said Dorothy. 'Well that's just what I'm looking for. Thank you.'

Fuzz began to look a bit more cheerful, and a sly twinkle entered his eyes as he replied 'Y'know, it's a funny thing but. . . .'

'Hold it!' interrupted Dorothy. 'We're not through yet. I'm not the only one that's come all this way to the land of Fuzz. There's this book and all its readers. You can't let them down.'

One of the boots stamped again. 'Oh, very well,' he spat. 'But you'll have to wait a minute.' He paused to blow his nose. Then from the end of his sleeve he pulled a long, wooden truncheon. He gave it a quick whirl round his head, and all at once it burst into a dazzling star as bright as a thousand sparklers. It burned for several minutes; and as it burned the whole chamber slipped into darkness so that only the glittering truncheon lit the room, casting flickering shadows behind the pillars and high into the vaulting. Then at last it flared into a final blaze of light, and with a 'pop' threw a myriad of sparks up into the air. Dorothy held her breath as slowly, slowly they drifted glittering to her feet. For as they gathered there, like so many glow-worms invited to a royal feast, she stood amazed at the shape they formed.

'Take it,' came Fuzz's voice, as from a great distance.

Dorothy stooped and took it, trembling. In her hand she had the most beautiful book she had ever seen. She turned the cover and on the first page she read. . . .

PART II

By gracious permission of

FUZZ

The Great and Terrible

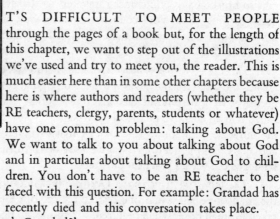

CHAPTER FIVE

Big Brother is Watching You

I T'S DIFFICULT TO MEET PEOPLE through the pages of a book but, for the length of this chapter, we want to step out of the illustrations we've used and try to meet you, the reader. This is much easier here than in some other chapters because here is where authors and readers (whether they be RE teachers, clergy, parents, students or whatever) have one common problem: talking about God. We want to talk to you about talking about God and in particular about talking about God to children. You don't have to be an RE teacher to be faced with this question. For example: Grandad has recently died and this conversation takes place.

'Mummy, where's Grandad?'

'He's gone away, dear.'

'Where?'

'God's taken him.'

'When's he coming back?'

'He won't be coming back. God's taken him away.'

'Mummy, will God take me away?'

This is already a theological discussion and a number of assumptions about God have been made by the mother and imparted to the child. God takes away people at whim; he won't let them come back; he is part and parcel of the tragedy of death. . . . Is it really surprising that 'God' is taboo in conversation?

Children mirror adult views of God (and adult views are often very 'childish' in the sense being of crude and undeveloped). Let's just think of a few of the ways in which the shorthand term 'God' is used by different people in conversation.

1. *The school caretaker image.* To many people God in relationship to the world is like the school caretaker and the school. He cares for it, in a rather un-obvious way. He works to promote its well-being, but can never be found. Any teacher reading this who's had a child sick on the classroom floor and tried to find the caretaker to get mopping-up operations in hand will appreciate this analogy! And like the caretaker who alleges he's on from 5 a.m., but always seems to be standing about – when he isn't needed – you suspect his integrity and ask whether you couldn't manage perfectly well without him (actually the analogy begins to break at this point since caretakers are harder to come by than head-teachers). Still, you see how this is the way in which some folk think about God, or at least their conversation implies that this is their picture of God.

2. *The super-intelligence image.* God stars in this as the Super Being who creates the universe and gives it order. In popular religion this survives perfectly well, despite the fact that philosophers such as Hume demolished it as an effective picture several centuries ago. But having created the universe God is not, fortunately, that involved in current events, and apart from generating a vague sense of warmth at Christmas, can be neglected for all practical purposes.

3. *The last nerve tonic image.* God is a pick-me-up. One reaches for the medicine shelf when one degree under. But God should only be taken in small doses when required. 'Caution – do not exceed the stated dose.' In other words, God and religion are very good things, provided you don't take them seriously. Addiction is dangerous.

4. *Big Brother.* If God is omniscient then he presumably sees you and knows your thoughts *all* the time. This could be awkward. We don't want this sort of prying. But there it is; rather uncomfortable. Big Brother is monitoring your every move, so watch it! The whole of life becomes a continuous assessment course with a final exam (death). If you pass, Heaven, but if not. . . .

5. *Jesus as God.* Despite NT refinements: 'What God was the Word was', 'Son of God' and the whole tendency to suggest that in Jesus God is uniquely at work, in some strands of popular thinking Jesus=God like 2+2=4. This at least makes God more human, but for some it

also puts him 2,000 years out of date and, as the Screwtape letters suggest, into a museum of togas and sandals and camels and lifeless waxworks.

6. *The experience image.* There are some forms of 'lower' experience, common to all men: hunger, desire to excrete, etc. There are also certain forms of 'higher' experience, open to all, but which for various reasons not all attain. Love is one example. After all, you never *see* love. You may see people kissing and rightly or wrongly think of it as love. Love means very little unless you experience it. God can be seen as belonging to this category of higher experience. You can, as with love, interpret certain events as God-directed or God-intended.

Of course there are other images, for example that of God as a Father Christmas figure, or the end-point in a manipulation system (you can work him by praying, performing certain tasks, being good). We've only listed a few and of course we aren't suggesting for a minute that those who hold them would necessarily articulate them in this manner. But we do want to say something about adult God-talk in general and it can be summed up quite briefly.

We all need images to help us to talk about any deep reality which transcends language. It is right and proper and natural to have recourse to images. But they can convey different things to different generations and eventually may have to be discarded. Ever since the Ten Commandments we've been warned not to worship images. The Jews' refusal even to name God (JHWH, for which they substituted 'the Lord') was a useful recognition that even to talk of God in human terms was in some sense to limit him.

So no image of God has a permanent, unchanging role – look at how the concept of father has changed since OT times – and all must be kept permanently under review. It follows, therefore, that in talking about God one must always consciously remember the shortcomings of the particular image one uses, or the context in which the word 'God' is used (an implied image). One must also remember its limitations and – in dialogue – ascertain what common ground there is. Does the same image convey the same association to the other person? Does he find a different image more meaningful? Can it be reconciled with ours? We believe a great deal of wasted discussion takes place on fruitless questions like 'Does God exist?', where more often than not the contenders are talking about utterly different images and so dialogue never occurs.

They never found their common ground by first enquiring in what ways it is proper to speak about God. But how does all this relate to children? Obviously it isn't possible or desirable for us to list a series of pat answers, lists of 'correct' things to say to children about God. We can, however, try to lay down some general guidelines.

1. First we must come to terms with ourselves and remember the fly's eye. The fly's eye has many windows set into it, all looking in at the same eye, but each from a different angle. Perhaps God is like the fly's eye, and the Victorian moral is not to try to tell someone else that their window isn't there because they can't see exactly what you can see in yours. There's a lot of myopia about.

2. The RE of the child should at some point deal with sign, symbol and imagery as a topic. This process can be started at primary level, and certainly should be considered in more depth in the secondary school, preferably soon after entry (if entry is at 11) and again at the post-13 or 14 age.

3. Older children should be encouraged to see the implications of their own God-talk so that they can see the images underlying their own thinking. They should also be introduced to images hitherto outside their background and perspective. This might mean a consideration of Jesus' talk about God, from parables and sayings, or the view of God in, say, Islam. Only then will they begin to see a lot that adults miss. The word 'telephone' conjures up a standard image for all of us; but children will learn that the term 'God' does not arouse such a simple or uniform response.

4. Adults should be extremely careful how they talk to children about God. Oversimplification does not help. Do we really think that contemporary children can write down 'God told Moses to bring the Hebrews out of Egypt' without asking why God doesn't work like that now, or for them, and wondering if the whole thing isn't a 'con', put about by adults to stop children questioning? On the other hand, 'Moses believed that God wanted him to take the Hebrews out of Egypt' is much better. First because it's neutral – an atheist can quite happily accept it. Second because it makes Moses more human; presumably he spent a lot of time wondering just what God did want, wrestling with doubt – as we might – but the biblical writer abbreviates all this in his account in order to get on to the point (for him) of God's mighty acts in bringing the Hebrews out of Egypt, and of the significance of the Exodus.

Anyway, before you get too suicidal about talking to children about God, remember, if we didn't talk about God with them at all we'd imply that the whole issue was of no importance and leave them to get more garbled versions from the newspapers, the 'Was God an astronaut?' writers, the doorstep vendors of canned religion and 'Stars on Sunday'. But remember, God is strictly to be handled with care.

CHAPTER SIX

Alice through the Blackboard

'EAR ME!' EXCLAIMED ALICE, 'HOW very vexing! That ledge is just fixed so that the chalk always rolls away under the blackboard where I can't reach it.'

She looked round for some more chalk. 'And that was my last piece. It really is *most* vexing. Well,' she said, making her mind up, 'there's nothing else for it: I shall simply have to get it back again.'

There was a crack between the ledge and the blackboard, so Alice squeezed her fingers through and wriggled them about to try to find the chalk. It was no good. She tried again in another place, but still could not find it.

'It must have rolled right behind the board. I wonder if I could reach it *this* way. . . .' And leaning forward against the blackboard she pushed through first a finger, then a hand, then a whole arm. It looked very black on the other side of the board, and she groped around for a while in the dark. Still she could not find the chalk, so she thrust her head and shoulder through as well. And then, all of a sudden – Bump!

'Ouch!'

She had fallen right through.

'However did that happen?' wondered Alice, frowning a little, for she was not accustomed to falling through blackboards. 'I suppose this must be Blackboard Land. And a queer sort of place it is – everything's in black and white, even me. And it's not the prettiest type of land-scape: there's only a blackboard and easel to look at. Otherwise it's just a huge black-and-white marble pavement stretching away for miles. If it weren't for this blackboard one could easily get lost.'

Alice decided she had seen all she wished of Blackboard Land, and began to speculate as to how she could get back to the classroom again.

'Perhaps if I go round to the other side of the board? Then maybe if I tried getting through *that* blackboard, the same thing would happen again, only in reverse.'

Alice got up and smoothed out her pinafore. Then she started to walk round to the front of the easel. But each time she was nearly there, the board dodged away and she had to start again. It was only when she had tied its legs together with her apron-strings that she got a good look at the front. But on the board somebody had written a poem. Alice paused to read it. It went like this:

PEDDAGOGGY

'Twas relig, and the writhy fourths
Did snipe and sniggle unbehave;
All dimsy was the Bible course
And the pedagogue outgrave.

'Beware the Bibliot, my son!
The voice that bores, the words that preach!
Beware the Tub-thub bird, and shun
The fundamous evangeteach.'

He took his coloured chalk in hand:
Long time the themic proach he taught –
So tested he the Bultmann key
And found the method caught.

And, as in trumpal words he wrote,
The Bibliot, with eyes aflame,
Came waffling with a bulgey note
Dictating as he came:

'I.2; 1.ii'; and through and through
Corinthians and Nehemiah,
Until at last he was out-classed
And firmly told 'Retire!'

> *'And hast thou sacked the Bibliot?*
> *Come to our class thou keenest man!*
> *O frabjous day! Callooh! Callay!*
> *Their jubilance began.*

> *'Twas relig, and the writhy fourths*
> *Did snipe and sniggle unbehave;*
> *All dimsy was the Bible course,*
> *And the pedagogue outgrave.*

'Well,' thought Alice, when she had finished reading it, 'I don't understand that poem very well at all. Somebody taught better than somebody else, that is clear; but I'm not sure about the rest. Anyway I think it's time I got back to my classroom.'

So saying, she walked up to the blackboard (which was now wriggling violently to untie itself) and jumped boldly through.

But she didn't find herself back in the classroom. Instead she was sitting on a patch of thistles just outside a dainty little gingerbread house.

'Help! Help! Let me out! Let me out this instant I say! Help! Help!' The screams were coming from a large bread-oven to one side of the yard.

'Goodness me!' Alice said to herself. 'This is just like the story of Hansel and Gretel. I bet that's the witch in the oven. Well, I'm jolly well going to let her out.'

She stepped over to the oven, and unlocked the heavy iron door. Out rolled a screaming black bundle.

'Help! Let me out! Open the door at once!' It continued to scream.

'Excuse me,' ventured Alice.

'Oh!' squeaked the bundle, unrolling itself and brushing off the cinders. 'Who are you? Things are becoming quite intolerable. It's not even twenty-four hours since I was last in that oven, and here I am in it again. I tell you, my patience is getting burned out. It's all the fault of those wretched, beastly children.'

'I expect they think you deserve it,' replied Alice, looking as stern as she could.

'And that just shows how ignorant you all are. Don't you realize how much good I've been doing them? Why I've been fattening them up for their end of term exams on a good, solid diet of Bible study.

And that's *bound* to do them good. We're on Deuteronomy already.'

'Are you sure that Deuteronomy is interesting enough for children?'

'It's the Word of God, and that's what counts,' parried the witch. 'We need to bring some faith back into this godless generation. Good, old-fashioned Bible study – that's what we need.'

Alice wondered whether making children read the Bible really would make them godly; and then she thought of all the important things it contained, and the problem seemed very difficult. But her thoughts were cut short by two fat children who rushed shouting out of the house.

'Now look what you've done! You've let her out – that's really ruined things. We'll be going back to all those dreadful lessons again!'

'But it was a bit mean to lock her in an oven,' pleaded Alice.

'Look what she does to us: first she locks us up in a classroom, and then she tortures us with Bible-reading. At least we only locked her up.'

'What's so terrible with Bible-reading?' •

'It's so boring! It wouldn't be half so bad if it made sense, or if it was in normal English, but it isn't. And in any case we don't want to be vicars. The sooner she gets back into that oven, the better. Come on, Gretel – let's fix her!'

Alice ran forward to help, but before she had taken two paces the ground beneath her opened, and she fell right into a trap.

It was being pulled by an old cart-horse, and sitting opposite her in the back were two cadaverous men in black top hats. They swayed to the motion of the trap.

'So glad you could drop in,' said one.

'Just how we hoped things would fall out,' added the other.

'Mr Chalk,' said the first, bowing politely.

'Mr Talk,' said the second, also bowing.

'And my name's Alice,' said Alice. 'Where are we going?'

'To the witch's tea party, of course. Everyone's going to be there, but everyone.'

'Which is why nobody's going,' explained Mr Talk.

Alice began to feel rather confused, and decided that she must have fallen through a credibility gap.

'Do you think the witch will be there?' she asked. 'I mean, will Hansel and Gretel have put her in the oven again?'

'She may drop in.'

'It depends how things fall out.'

'Well, I feel very sorry for her, always being pushed into the oven like that.'

'Now there I take issue with you,' exclaimed Mr Chalk. 'The whole point is that her teaching methods are half-baked. She's a Bibliot.'

'Stuck in the Bible all the time,' added Mr Talk. 'It simply isn't suitable.'

'Why not?' asked Alice.

'Oh, for many reasons,' Mr Chalk explained. 'To start with, she hasn't realized the psychological problems. You have only to mention the Bible, almost, and children will think they are being preached at. And what sort of image has the Bible got? An Old Testament full of fairy-tales and gibberish, and a New Testament all about a sickly, Sunday-school Jesus. The image has to be destroyed before the reality can step out; but mere reading isn't enough to do that.'

Alice looked blank.

'No, indeed,' chimed in Mr Talk. 'Because the Bible is very much an adult book. It was written as works for adults, by adults. And its age and complexity makes it hard even for adults to understand nowadays. What children need is a lively presentation which isn't tied down to the text. This applies especially to slow learners for whom the Bible, taken neat, is even more inappropriate than for any others.'

'And then there are the philosophical problems.' Mr Chalk was warming to his theme. 'She hopes that Hansel and Gretel will absorb faith through Bible-reading. But isn't she assuming a willingness to believe which may not be there? Perhaps a sounder approach would be to disregard her own beliefs and concentrate on educating her pupils to think about religion with sensitivity and interest. This at least agrees with sound educational aims.'

'Don't forget to mention the practical problems,' put in Mr Talk.

'I'm not forgetting; but I'd just like to point out that Bible-reading in schools has not, after all, produced more Christians. Look at the churches: half empty, or worse. But part of the problem lies in the Bible itself. Parts of it contain stories going back as far as four thousand years. They deal with strange lands, strange ways of life, strange beliefs sometimes. Much of the Bible is dauntingly unfamiliar. And it embodies so many different types of literature, from folk-tale to complex theological argument;[1] so many different authors, so many outlooks, so many unsuspected difficulties and subtleties. Just to teach the Bible as a

1. See Chapter 12 on the Bible and mythology.

straightforward story-book is to confuse the children and debase the Bible.'

'You make it sound very difficult to use the Bible at all.'

'It has to be used with discretion.'

'Well, I wish you'd suggest some solutions,' said Alice, who by now was growing very impatient.

'You'll have to seek expert advice on that, I'm afraid,' said Mr Talk.

'Who do you suggest?'

'Ah, now there's a question! Who do we suggest?' and Mr Chalk puffed himself up importantly. 'I suggest that we appoint a Royal Commiseration.'

'That's nonsense,' said Alice, 'You can't; and anyway you're not royal.'

'No. She's right,' said Mr Talk. 'It'll have to be the Penguin.'

'The Penguin?' spluttered Mr Chalk, turning purple with indignation. 'The Penguin, you say? The Penguin would be altogether unsuitable, and is quite out of the question.'

'Unsuitable?' Mr Talk was now beginning to shout too. Alice saw that at any minute they would stand up in the trap and roll up their sleeves for a fight, so she quickly interposed.

'Well can you suggest a third alternative?'

'The Good Knight, without a doubt.'

'The Good Knight?' Alice hadn't heard him mentioned before.

'Yes, the Good Knight.'

'Good Knight!'

'Good Night.'

And the two men fell asleep.

When Alice found the Good Knight, he was sitting in his cave mouth planting out carrots and marking in their positions on his map of the world.

'Now,' said the Good Knight, as he drew a large cross over Birmingham, 'You want to know how to use the Bible in class. Well, you've heard that you can't use it as a story-book, and you've heard why. But there are several ways in which it is of first importance as source-material.'

He loosened his greaves and took a close look at the continent. 'Number One,' he enunciated firmly, planting a carrot in Hamburg. 'You can use the Bible to illustrate how religions have developed. It has splendid documentation for nomadic beliefs, the religions of city states, the growth of temples and priesthoods, of the development of prophecy; there are outstanding examples of religious leaders, the birth of a new religion, its growth to an organized movement, the impact of persecution. It also has source-material for studying the development of individual religious concepts such as faith, or the nature of God, or salvation.

'Then Number Two' (Cairo was demolished), 'you can select material from the Bible to make comparisons with other religions. Myths, religious practices, laws, beliefs, types of literature, types of leader – these are common to most religions. How far does the Bible illustrate a common pattern?

'But, Number Three' (and here a carrot dived into the Indian Ocean), 'don't forget that it can also be used to illustrate the distinctive elements of Jewish and Christian beliefs: the idea of a God who acts and makes moral demands, or gives up his own godhead to help his creatures.

'And also Number Four,' continued the Knight, using yet another carrot to obliterate New South Wales, 'older children need to be shown the textual complexity involved in ancient documents. They need to know about the problems that arise from oral transmission and textual corruption. Parts of the Bible can be used to illustrate these themes in a representative way for the Bible as a whole. Younger children, on the other hand, can be introduced to selections of the Bible to illustrate the varying types of literature it contains. This gives them an insight into what religious literature really is.'

'What you seem to be saying,' hazarded Alice, 'is that it is best to use the Bible as a source-book, but not as an end in itself.'

'That's exactly right. Even where a thoroughly biblical topic has to be taught, such as the Life of Christ, it is unwise to use the Bible as a textbook. Children find it much more stimulating if the topic is presented in a lively way by themes, perhaps through story-telling or drama by the teacher.'

'But you think it would be all right to pick out an individual story from the Bible, to illustrate a theme?'

'Yes, and it's better enacted than read,' replied the Knight, blocking the Panama Canal. 'But one thing is very important: study the story beforehand in a good commentary. Each one can have many levels of meaning.'

'I don't understand,' said Alice.

'Well, first of all we have to think of the original events of the story. What significance did the original participants see in them? Then maybe the story was preserved in oral tradition for some years before it was written down. Did the story-tellers see in it the same significance as the original participants? Did they perhaps add on a moral to sum it up? Or emphasize a particular aspect? Then at some stage it was written down. The writer too may have seen a slightly different significance in the story, and adapted it a little, or put it in a new context to bring out the meaning it held for him. And sometimes we even get one or two more phases where later editors have rearranged earlier books into schemes of their own. They too may have had different ideas. So sometimes there can be as many as four or five meanings to a biblical story, even before a modern reader has tried to see a meaning in it for himself.'

'Goodness!' Alice exclaimed.

'Ah, but you can't use them all. It would confuse your pupils. Your job is to select the meaning that illustrates your theme, and not to mix up the different strata.'

But Alice had been gradually wandering into the cave. 'Mix up what, did you say?' she asked from the semi-darkness.

'Select the meaning that illustrates your theme, and . . . .' The Knight's voice came only faintly as Alice walked deeper into the gloom. She supposed that the Knight must by now have turned at least New York, Madrid and Moscow into world carrot-centres. The darkness was so deep that she had to feel ahead with her fingers and toes. She came to a wall. It led off to the left, and as she followed it, it rounded a corner. In a small lighted chamber she found herself faced by a large blackboard, which stood on an easel in the middle of the room. Alice moved towards it, again thinking that it might provide her with a route home. But as she looked there appeared on the clean board, one by one as if being written by an invisible hand, a series of chalk-written letters which formed an inscription:

Welcome
to
Part III

CHAPTER SEVEN

Take One

AS FAR AS CHILDREN ARE CONCERNED the church is played out, or rather that's the impression that any discussion will give you, since those who go to church are usually silent through fear of being laughed at, or through doubt. So that often the RE teacher finds himself playing devil's advocate in defending the church, and by so doing runs perilously close to becoming a vicar figure in the eyes of the children. At the same time anyone who has ever been in a secondary school classroom will know that as a topic 'the church' probably excites more crass stupidity, arrant nonsense and pre-senile drivel from children by way of 'opinion' than any other, most often from those who've never been near a church. So how has this all arisen and by what means should it be challenged?

Whereas the present generation of parents tends to view the church as a 'good thing', even though for all practical purposes it can go to hell, the present generation of children are (albeit still apathetically) more 'anti'. To them – or rather the vociferous ones – the church stands for old age, irrelevance, authoritarianism and cant. To many it's not even a force to be reckoned with. We invite you to think of factors that might account for this. Pause here for thought.

We think the following have been contributory:

1. *The effect of bad school assemblies.* For many children this is their only experience of worship – and it can be worthless.

2. *The church's public image.* Too often the building *does* look dilapidated, the congregation musty, too often they seem 'agin' modern society. How far this is the real, or general picture is another question.

3. *The desire to test the teacher*. Children may be hostile simply because they're trying the RE teacher, to see if he is a missionary in disguise who will rush to defend mother church. And they've caught out a good few this way. . .

4. *The adolescent rejection phase*. The attitude of young people to the church could be part of their rejection phase, e.g. of school as an institution, of parents: healthy, growing, temporary flexing of muscles against the society they've inherited.

5. *Reaction against hypocrisy*. They see through the hypocrisy – or if you want to be more mealy-mouthed, inconsistency – of parents paying lip-service to the church, but with no real interest or commitment.

6. *The church's failure to speak out enough on social and political issues*. Personally we aren't sure how hard to push this point. Some people feel very bitter about the church's lack of an authoritative voice. Some interpret this as a genuine call to individual faith to cope with life's problems without removal of decision-making responsibility. Others see this as a time for the church to set its own house in order, rather than tell 'the world' how to live. Anyhow, to what extent a plea for some sort of spirituality in an age of materialism would be heeded we don't know.

7. *The influence of submerged guilt*. On the question of the church many non-aligned notional Christians (C of E on application forms) have a host of excuses for non-commitment. Let's not confuse these with reasons. One excuse may be that the church holds boring services, but the reason may be that the speaker may very well want to live as a materialist, and wash his car on Sunday mornings while hanging on to the nominal Christianity that believes in helping others, especially at Christmas. A great deal of the anti-church barrage is, we believe, a set of excuses rather than reasons. Of course the excuses might be good; church services may be boring. The fact remains that often they cover deep and unarticulated reasons. In our society all of us are to a greater or lesser extent materialist in outlook but some of us do weird and wonderful mental gymnastics to marry this with a religious outlook.

There's a lot of food for thought in those seven points and one could add others. One thing clearly emerges: the RE teacher preparing to tackle the church with older children is in very deep waters indeed – can he walk on them and survive?

'Lights!' Cameras!'
'Okay, you guys, Take One.'
'Take One.'
'Take One.'
The scene: a budget production of the new dime epic 'A Day in the Life of an RE teacher'. Enter the star, J. Grupert Heinkler Jr. He faces a class of fourth-year children (actually extras borrowed from *The Bible*, *The Ten Commandments*, etc. Some are getting on in years and wear hearing-aids, wigs, while others have wooden legs or glass eyes.) The action starts. The teacher perches on the end of his desk, an attempt at informality which causes near-rupture. He smiles painfully.
'Good morning, children. Today we're going to discuss the church.'
Indifference from the extras.
'Now what's wrong with it?'
'It's a bore.' Blue-eyed blonde Sylvia Sexpool (40-26-38), teeny-bopper star in gym-slip – the camera moves in to make the most of this.
'No it isn't.' J. Grupert Heinkler Jr fighting to keep the class and get them to his way of thinking, and also trying to get camera 2 back on himself.
'No good, you guys, cut!'

'Lights! Cameras!'
'Okay, you guys, roll 'em.'
'Take Two.'
'Take Two.'
Camera pans in on Grupert.
'Good morning, children. Today ...' and action proceeds. It continues until Grupert's line:
'I can think of lots of good things the church has done. Here's a textbook full of them.' Boohs, yahs, catcalls, groans. Camera 1 scans class and picks up Sylvia who is making a face at the teacher. But calamity! She has forgotten to stub out the cigar she lit after the last take. So the director again intervenes:
'No good, cut!'

'Okay, you guys, before we Take Three we gotta getta betta script.'
Writers Glasseyekov and Lavatour are called in. They try various approaches: scripting Grupert to write a list of often heard comments,

remarks and questions on 'the church' on the blackboard, as a way in
to group discussion. Each of these comments could lead into a whole
series of discussion follow-up lessons, e.g.:

> Sermons are not the best way to get through to congregations.
> Hymn words and tunes are out of date.
> The qualifications for a good priest/vicar/minister would be. . . .
> The church's main function seems to be. . . .
> The church's main function ought to be. . . .

Scripting allows discussion of whether the question itself is loaded,
presupposing a certain answer, and props supply the relevant support
materials, tapes of modern hymns and hymn tunes (such as those by
Sydney Carter), handouts produced by different churches (such as the
excellent series by the Salvation Army). The script men now reach a
vital conclusion: the most critical factor is the degree of sensitivity
which Grupert as the teacher can bring to the discussion. Can he carry
this approach, or would a real-life class lynch him?

Take Four. They try another line: the class are introduced to the topic
by a survey of local churches in their own area. They are asked a number of questions which depend on their attending a church service.
This helps an informed discussion; of course it has to be a voluntary
activity since no teacher has the power to force his class to go to church,
but in practice many are keen to go along with their list of questions.
Those who choose not to can contribute with a useful survey on
hymns, based on the school hymnbook. The group is thus given a
practical task, which they can use as the basis for discussion, and a mass
results chart for the wall can then be produced by volunteers. If the
teacher is nervous of the approach in the previous script he can try this,
since not quite the same sensitivity is required on his part in this second
approach. It also means that some of the most unlikely members of the
group will actually defend some of the activities of the church and
save the teacher from acting the double role of vicar figure.

Take Five. They try scripting another idea: the outside speaker. Not
used as a boring lecturer but as the subject of a firing squad of questions,
posed by the group and on their own wavelength, prepared in advance.
Contrasting personalities are chosen as outside speakers: the RC priest,
Baptist minister, etc., not to bang the denominational drum but to
answer questions about the church and their own tradition. But not

all can switch on to the wavelength of the group quickly; the personality of the visitor is a key factor.

Take Six. Group work study cards are tried next, from CEM's range on the church. The writers discover that this technique only interests the extras if they've first been interested by a provocative introductory class lesson/lessons. And Sylvia spends all her time in her group talking about boyfriends, which means that unless the teacher's breathing down her neck she isn't working.

Their conclusion: a good script is vital or, in our RE terms, planning and choice of material are each of utmost importance. But nothing we can suggest will really make a bad teacher good, since the root of bad teaching is insensitivity, and insensitive teachers don't think they need to learn anything. If like us you have been or are in the situation of the RE teacher faced with the church as an inevitable topic, then each approach posed above could work, depending, of course, on observing and trying to meet the limitations of each, and depending very much on you and your ability to elicit comment, provoke thought and come to terms with your own pro- or anti-church feeling. In the studio of the school and the set of the classroom you are director and probably principal actor. Props may be in short supply. If yours is a budget production, you may have to manage on very few, but remember these cardinal rules:

1. Be aware of the depth of the problem of 'church and classroom' as we've discussed it in the first half of this chapter.

2. Children (and adults) must grasp that the nature of church lies in Christian community, its life and service, rather than in particular institutional expressions of this in a particular denomination or set of buildings. Here we move into theology.

3. Be resilient enough to try several of these suggested approaches. Eventually you should find the one best suited to you, that plunges your children into an informed discussion of this question without making you into an out-of-work vicar trying to force his claim on a reluctant dole queue.

So much for the church, or at least for the moment. What about the allied problem, worship? Obviously it's got a lot in common with the church as a teaching problem. More difficult, as any adult knows, you can attend a church service and not experience worship. A whole tradition of RE books (for teachers and pupils) takes the line that you understand worship by worshipping (they've obviously heard of learning by doing), so you're encouraged to plunge your children into Sikh worship, Moslem prayers, Catholic Mass and whatever so they can feel its point. There's a whole multi-racial bandwaggon to be jumped on here.

But before you leap off let's share some reservations with you. If you can take children to a Sikh temple, well and good. More often teachers try to create the atmosphere in school assembly. Let's be honest, they aren't kidding anybody. Imitations don't get into the spirit of the thing, any more than assemblies that try to ape church services.

And if you let your children see or be part of real worship it will mean nothing unless they understand the nature of worship, which is where you are vital, because many textbooks provide descriptions, pictures of worship in different situations and religions – few discuss what worship is. Go back with children – maybe with yourself – to the roots of the whole thing:

(a) The basic human need for ritual. Not only does ritual help to regularize daily life (please, thank you, Dear Sir, one ding for stop) and have a therapeutic value (putting the kettle on, or an infant's burial service for a deceased pet, or aaatchooo – bless you!), it seems basic to almost all religion. After all, even the most 'anti-ritualistic' nonconformist church *has* a ritual. Its minister wears ordinary garments, no clerical collar, and its churches have no crosses, statues or whatever. And like all ritual it *says* something about the beliefs of the people who use it – in this case it's a statement about the nature of Christian ministry.

(b) Worship is a ritual affirmation of the values we hold dear: the Christian at church and the materialist washing his (often perfectly clean) car both say 'yes' to certain values by their actions.

(c) In another sense worship opens one to receive inspiration from one's source of values: the Quaker in his silence and the Catholic in the pageant of High Mass both receive inspiration from what they agree to be the source of their affirmations – God. And worship is intended to be communion with the source, made easier by the ritual and the leader of worship, whether he be priest or lay, man or woman.

(d) So through dramatic re-enactment (as at Communion services) of past events we interpret our present, and we are given a 'part' in the drama. We sing, say, do certain things which remember the past, interpret the present and point to the future.

Now if no one explained to you this drama of the meaning of life, or the part you are challenged to play, surprise could hardly be expressed at a hostile or negative reaction if you were to be plunged into 'worship'. It may be that we all need to worship (albeit in different ways, or to different 'sources') : we owe it to children first to try to lay bare the bones of worship, then to show them all the marvellous textbook examples, or to discuss variants. So again the lesson series should have a good, clear introductory lesson/lessons on the nature of worship to provoke them, then blossom into examples, and have a good, clear summary lesson/lessons to bring all this together in the light of their experiences and thinking.

The Air from Handel's *Water Music* daintily introduces Dame Florid Melstrom as the camera moves in towards her. She smiles – leers – at it sickeningly. Cameraman blanches.

'Welcome to *Startime on Sunday*,' she chokes emotionally, 'where great stars will share with you songs and hymns that (eyeballs roll) have meaning.' She clasps her handkerchief, pats the pug dog on her lap and the camera turns to focus on a large rubber plant as strains of 'Jerusalem' increase. Dame Florid grins sardonically.

'Yes, we have the comfort of the church; isn't it a good thing? While you sit at home watching this in your millions the church carries on, er, its work' (servile smile, pausing to polish her glass eye she continues), 'so let us hear this noble hymn, which gives us so much comfort. . . .' Fade into

> Till we have built Jerusalem
>
> In England's green and pleasant land.

While the camerman is carried off, ask yourself: will the next generation continue to equate this cosy sentimentality with Christian belief and churchmanship? Or will RE at least make people question the position which they have uncritically accepted in the past? For although it is no part of the brief of the RE teacher to defend the church, his concern for the phenomenon of religion as a whole must lead him to ask the question whether the public image of the church will stand analysis and investigation.

Further help for the teacher

Suggested teacher's aim

To encourage children to examine (*a*) the nature of the church, i.e. community, (*b*) their own image of the church, in the light of selected material and experience.

Academic background for the teacher

(*a*) *Introductory*

John Bowden, *Who is a Christian?*, SCM Press 1970; R. P. C. Hanson (ed.), *Difficulties for Christian Belief*, Macmillan 1967, essay by John Bowden, 'The Church', pp. 122–49; Kenneth Slack, *The British Churches Today*, SCM Press 1970; Victor de Waal, *What about the Church?* SCM Press 1969.

(*b*) *Advanced*

For reference: F. L. Cross and E. A. Livingstone (eds.), *The Oxford Dictionary of the Christian Church*, second edition, OUP 1974; K. L. Schmidt, *The Church* (Bible Key Words), A. & C. Black 1950.

For an introduction to 'fringe' sects: Horton Davies, *Christian Deviations*, fourth edition, SCM Press 1972.

For use in comparison with earlier forms of church: J. Daniélou and H. Marrou, *The First Six Hundred Years*, Darton Longman Todd 1964; Norman Sykes, *The English Religious Tradition*, SCM Press 1953; J. W. C. Wand, *A History of the Early Church*, Methuen 1963.

Useful material for the classroom

Ian H. Birnie: a series called Focus on Christianity, but especially vol. 1, *The Church in Your Community*, and vol. 5, *The Church in the Third World*, Edward Arnold 1969; CEM Workcards: *Discovering the Church* (ten cards and teacher's handbook) are useful at CSE level, also the CEM Factfinder, *Christians and Churchgoing*.

This is a topic in which outside speakers can be very useful. It is important to remember the general problems of the use of outside speakers as expressed in Chapter 2, and in this particular topic it is also worth noting that getting members of the local clergy to beat denominational drums is neither an exercise they welcome, nor is it the best use of their visit from the children's point of view. Much better to discuss with the class in advance what you want to get out of the speaker: Why does he think the church is worth belonging to? What problems does he see in connection with services? And so on. Prepare the questions, as a group, in advance so that no long silences waste the time of the visit. Avoid a talk by the speaker; he may spend three-quarters of the period on this and fail to get on the right wavelength of the group's interests and feelings. Having to answer direct questions on matters that concern them brings him into far more profitable use – he is after all what educationalists would term a resource. Sometimes it pays to get two speakers (at different times) to answer the same questions. Always it pays for the children to prepare their questions in advance, but of course this doesn't preclude supplementaries. You should always be as inconspicuous as possible during the visit; your group don't want to hear you at all. You can even arrange for members of the group to meet the speaker on his arrival in the school, guide him or her to the classroom, and a group member might chair the meeting. In this case he/she would need to be carefully chosen and primed in advance on the duties of chairman. The advantage of all this? It encourages a more adult approach in the group and makes the speaker *their* guest. In discussion-orientated work the visiting speaker can be the spice of life. Choose him well, by personality not views! Make clear to him in advance what his role will be. See that your head-teacher is aware of his visit (it's not good for public relations to have strangers wandering round the school), and see that any expenses are paid. Otherwise your speaker may not come again!

A specimen questionnaire for a survey of the local church

Name of church
Denomination
Date and time of service
Approx. seating capacity
No. of people present
No. of females
% of females
No. under 18
% under 18
No. 18–50
No. 50+

No. of (*a*) hymns, (*b*) psalms. Did they fit in with the theme of
the service and the sermon?

What readings were used?

What was the subject of the sermon?

How long did the sermon last?

Was the preacher a visitor or the resident vicar/priest/minister?

(If you were a visitor) Was the congregation friendly to out-
siders? From the notices (written or on the board) what evidence
did you see of (*a*) weekday (*b*) weeknight activities? List the
main ones.

Did you feel the service boring/lively/helpful/difficult to follow/
surprising/inspiring/clear? Cross out words which don't apply.
If none of these words apply, how would you sum up the
service you surveyed?

Add more comments if you wish.

A note on this survey

Obviously no real attempt is being made here to produce a sound
statistical analysis of churchmanship in a given area, though a different
questionnaire could be produced to investigate this. The aim here is to
get the group to look at a service critically (in the proper sense of the
word) and to give them and the teacher a good base in experience on
which to build class discussion. The teacher can then elucidate their
findings on prayer used or ritual. They will need to compare answers,
to be questioned further on some of them, especially those involving
subjective judgment. Where two people attended the same service the
answers received may be different: those concerned should have opportunity to compare and discuss together why they reached different
conclusions.

Visits to churches during school hours to interview the clergy can also
be used to enrich the experience of the class. If the class can be dispersed
to, say, four different churches (but to ask broadly similar questions),
there can be useful comparison; interviews could be tape-recorded. But
as with the visit to the school by an outside speaker, group preparation
and post-visit evaluation are as important as the encounter itself. Timetable permutations might not permit a trip out to interview out of
school – though if geography can have trips out in lesson time we don't
see why RE shouldn't – but at any event the RE teacher must, to do

justice to the church as a topic, make some use of local, living material. The question might arise as to what to do if local material is poor. There is no absolute solution to this, though it must be used sparingly and (this applies whatever the 'quality') children must not be encouraged to over-generalize from a limited sample. Bring in speakers from further afield in a case such as this, and be prepared to travel further for survey purposes, so that at least good and bad are seen.

CHAPTER EIGHT

Saturday Night is Vampire Night

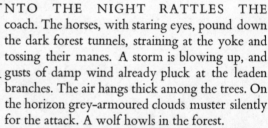

INTO THE NIGHT RATTLES THE coach. The horses, with staring eyes, pound down the dark forest tunnels, straining at the yoke and tossing their manes. A storm is blowing up, and gusts of damp wind already pluck at the leaden branches. The air hangs thick among the trees. On the horizon grey-armoured clouds muster silently for the attack. A wolf howls in the forest.

Set on a black rock rising sheer out of the forest, Castle Dracula cuts into the pale sky. From somewhere amidst the buttresses and turrets comes the thin chime of a clock. Midnight. Deep in the bowels of the castle something stirs. . . .

In the stalls Daphne reaches out a hand for reassurance.

The thunder claps and the lightning hisses. In a sudden flash the drooling vampire rises exultant with a flap of his wings, and drops into flight from a turret window. . . .

On the way home the shadows outside the fish and chip shop lie in wait for the young couple, and threaten them with un-nameable horrors. The supernatural lurks round the corner of Primrose Lane. In the policeman's steady footfall they hear the undead stalking them to the porch of 32 Railway Terrace, Bradford, Yorks.

A temporary belief in the after-life can readily be evoked, from pulpit or screen or printed page, by those with the skill to speak to our deeper fears and to manipulate our emotions. These techniques have no place in the classroom, where the aim should not be to arouse or instil a belief in life after death, but to expound the different beliefs concerning it, and to discuss their implications and the grounds for belief or disbelief in them.

On the other hand, if we want to avoid immediate and unthinking dismissal of the subject, our common experience of the unease produced by ghost-stories can sometimes provide a starting-point for a lesson or lesson-series on the subject of life after death. Why do ghost-stories and Dracula films give us the creeps? Is there a latent belief in the after-life in anyone who can be frightened by them? And if they produce, or play on, belief, is this the same quality or kind of belief that is involved in Buddhist, Hindu or Christian ideas?

One of the aims of teaching this topic should be to show children the great variety of concepts of the after-life and to destroy the notion, often prevalent, that all religions hold a uniform picture into which God, the resurrection, heaven, hell, ghouls, vampires, ouija boards and Dennis Wheatley all fit. Our task, as always, is to assist our pupils to-wards a greater theological maturity. So in the course of discussion it is desirable to introduce careful explanations of, for example, the concept of nirvana, or of reincarnation. It is also, in our view, important to break down the impression that Christian teaching concerning the after-life has always been a monolithic doctrine of heaven and hell. The terms 'heaven' and 'hell' need to be discussed. They have held different connotations for different people, and these can be illustrated from art, music and literature. And when the Fourth Gospel speaks of 'eternal life' as something available in the present, how far does this modify the traditional view of 'heaven' as a place or state to which we are introduced by the undertaker?

There is also the disagreement within the Christian tradition between the universalist view – that a loving God will ultimately save all men – and other views: of predestination, or of ledger-book judgment, or of Hell as a self-imposed fate which man chooses when he freely rejects God. Within the Bible itself one can see a variety of views concerning the after-life, and perhaps a process of development, from ambiguous passages in the Old Testament to Paul's affirmation in I Corinthians. A principal aim, then, should be to widen the range of the term 'after-life'. Until this is done all discussion on the subject will be prejudiced, ignorant and worthless.

With the wider background you can then introduce wider issues, and a discussion on the after-life can develop into an attempt to define religious belief and how it differs from superstition. Does a belief in the Headless Coachman of Devizes carry the same moral implications as a belief in the communion of saints or in reincarnation? And does a belief in Nirvana imply the same evaluation of life as the Johannine teaching on 'eternal life'? Attitudes towards death can affect the way people live, and attitudes towards life can affect people's view of death. It is misleading to try to consider the question of an after-life in isolation, and your pupils need to be aware of this. The degree to which the two affect one another may provide us with an index for distinguishing between superstition and religious belief.

Inevitably the question will arise whether there really is an after-life. An attempt to answer this question in the classroom, whether by discussion or by sermon, is not likely to be fruitful. For one thing you certainly will not answer the question finally; and for another you will not greatly advance or deepen the pupils' understanding of the problems involved. Better instead to take one step back and discuss how far such a discussion could take one to a solution.

Your pupils should ask themselves what sort of evidence they could use which might help to decide the issue. There are the claims from spiritualists and the experiences of people who have been to séances. Rather than discuss these in the abstract it is better to take a written account as a case-study, and analyse in class the adequacy or inadequacy of its evidence. Here again it is the teacher's job to feed material into the discussion. Then also some of the Greek philosophers based their belief on philosophical considerations: the reasoning soul embodied in each human individual was a part of a universal and eternal Reason. The soul was, therefore, by definition immortal. Can a philosophical system prove that there is life after death? Or that there is not? Then there is the mass of evidence, archaeological as well as documentary, that among all men at all times there seems to have been a belief in life after death. Does the persistence of the idea of an after-life indicate the truth of the idea? And if not, how does one account for its origin and prevalence? And how in practice might one distinguish between wishful thinking, intuitive insight and spiritual illumination? Some people hold that the best evidence comes from the Bible, and especially from the account of Jesus' resurrection. How straightforward is the evidence here? By what sort of standards can one judge the probability of the two New Testament traditions of Jesus' appearances after his death and the empty tomb?

The difficulty, which children should be made to appreciate, is that on a subject such as this there is no indisputable evidence. What is brought forward by one person as evidence can be rejected by another according to the disposition of each to accept or reject belief in an after-life. To highlight this impasse is an important task for the teacher, as to do so forms a constructive step in teaching children to think about religion. You can turn it to good use, for maybe (according to many theologians and philosophers) it is the character of the supernatural that it can never be deduced from the natural.

How widely and deeply this topic is explored must depend on the time available, and on the age and intellectual capacity of the class. With eleven-year-olds one would concentrate mostly on widening their understanding of the term 'after-life', for which a pictorial presentation is very suitable. With older children greater emphasis can be placed on discussion. Conclusions 'in favour' of life after death or 'against' it should not be sought and certainly should not be imposed. Instead, the discussion should be an open-ended investigation into the issues involved in the topic. Conclusions can be drawn on *how* to think about life after death, but not on *what* to think about it. That must be left to your pupils.

Further help for the teacher

Suggested teacher's aim

(*a*) To widen children's understanding of the term 'after-life' by examining and comparing beliefs and practices of various religions, past and present; in so doing to help them to acquire critical evaluation techniques for the handling of the material.

(*b*) To examine how far it is appropriate to seek to prove or disprove the reality of an after-life.

(*c*) *NOT* to seek to prove or disprove it for them.

Academic background for the teacher

(*a*) *Introductory*

This is a very wide-ranging topic, and will probably involve dipping into a large number of books.

For archaeological background: *New Larousse Encyclopaedia of Mythology*, Hamlyn 1959; Index, 'Burial Customs', in S. Piggott (ed.), *The Dawn of Civilisation*, Thames & Hudson 1962.

For other modern world religions: L. Aletrino, *Six World Religions*, SCM Press 1968; B. W. Sherratt and D. J. Hawkins, *Gods and Men*, Blackie 1972. The latter provides a useful general bibliography of each religion treated. As a quicker primer for the teacher it is probably the best world religions book in one volume, and could be used at sixth-form General Studies level.

For Christianity: Karl Barth, *Dogmatics in Outline*, SCM Press 1949, pp. 153ff.; C. S. Lewis, *The Great Divorce*, Bles 1946, Fontana 1972: as a parable this makes excellent reading – certainly sixth-formers could read it for themselves; A. R. Vidler, *Christian Belief*, SCM Press 1950, ch. 7.

For Spiritualism: Horton Davies, *Christian Deviations*, fourth edition, SCM Press 1972.

For philosophy: references to immortality in Bertrand Russell, *History of Western Philosophy*, Allen & Unwin 1961 and a useful follow-up in R. H. Popkin, A. Stroll, A. V. Kelly, *Philosophy Made Simple*, W. H. Allen 1956.

(b) Advanced

Archaeology: H. Carter, *The Tomb of Tutankhamen*, Sphere 1972; E. A. W. Budge, *The Book of the Dead*, *The Papyrus of Ani*, Vol. I, Warner 1913; C. L. Woolley, *Excavations at Ur*, Ernest Benn 1954.

World religions: C. Humphreys, *Buddhism*; K. M. Sen, *Hinduism*; A. Guillaume, *Islam*, Penguin 1951, 1961, 1954 respectively.

Judaism: W. Eichrodt, *Theology of the Old Testament*, Vol. II, SCM Press 1967, chs. XIX, XXIV.

Christianity: C. H. Dodd, *The Interpretation of the Fourth Gospel*, CUP 1953, pp. 144ff.; J. A. T. Robinson, *In the End God*, Fontana 1968; J. N. D. Kelly, *Early Christian Doctrines*, A. & C. Black 1958, ch. XVII; O. C. Quick, *Doctrines of the Creed*, Nisbit 1938, chs. XII, XIII, XIV.

Spiritualism: Ena Twigg, with Ruth Hagy-Brod, *Ena Twigg: Medium*, W. H. Allen 1974.

Materials for the classroom

This is one of the (almost unlimited) areas poorly supported by commercially-produced teaching aids in RE. Ghost stories are not hard to come by, and those of M. R. James are particularly recommended, by contrast with some of the less subtle spook thrillers currently available in the pulp press. 'True' ghost stories, also, can be collected from local and national press, magazines and anthologies. Local libraries can also be helpful here. The teacher's role, having amassed material of this sort, and involved children in its collection, is to help them to evaluate it critically. Is there more about the data in question that has to be known before it can be verified? How have the interest of the writer and the readership affected the selection of material and its presentation? Would it satisfy a scientist? Are there alternative explanations?

The archaeological and ethnographical material is often suitable for illustration. Good board-work with plenty of colour must be the first preference. But slides, pre-drawn overhead projector material and photographs make a fair second. Ward Lock Educational have been producing (1970 onwards) a Living Religions Series. These booklets provide useful information for the more able child, and in several cases for the teacher: the ones on Judaism, Islam, Hinduism, Buddhism and Humanism can be used here, but they are all worth getting to know in terms of any teaching you have to do on world religions.

Where textual material is available from religious writings, ancient and modern, it can be convenient to bring these together into one duplicated pamphlet. If the teacher wishes, these can be converted into worksheets by the addition of carefully composed questions. Pictorial material illustrating concepts of heaven and hell is not hard to find. The Old Masters are well represented in coffee-table books and posters, and are easily available at public libraries. The work of Bosch, in particular, is so frequently reproduced as to be something of a cliché. In addition attention may be drawn to mediaeval wall-paintings which often depict heaven and hell.

From literature, Dante's *Divine Comedy* must be the supreme illustrative example. For more advanced pupils it is also possible to consider J.-P. Sartre's *Huis Clos* as a classic modern interpretation of hell, demythologized.

In music, various attitudes towards the significance of life after death are dramatically and sometimes poignantly represented in Brahms' *A German Requiem, short* sections of which would be useful illustrative material for the classroom.

To treat a section of spiritualist writing as a case-study can be profitable. It is helpful to duplicate the relevant passage before attempting to discuss it, if it is of any length. With the contemporary boom in occultism it should not be hard to find source material in libraries and bookshops. The autobiography of Ena Twigg is recommended merely as a 'starter'.

It is important for children to understand not only 'views' about an after-life in their final form (speaking in earthly terms!) but also to see how they developed over a period of time. Obviously the Hebrew-Jewish view is one whose development is well-documented. Bible dictionaries under 'Death', 'Sheol', 'Soul' and inter-connected references will provide a sketch of the development.

General Points

Death is a subject which preoccupies children far more than adults normally suppose or like to suppose. The teacher can easily cash in on this ready-made interest, but must be scrupulously careful not to do so in a way which panders to the gruesome, the emotional or the sentimental. In Britain alone attitudes have changed a lot in the last hundred years; see J. S. Curl, *The Victorian Celebration of Death*, David and Charles 1972, as one example – a study of Victorian burial grounds! – of ways of approach to this topic. Sensitivity on the part of the teacher is called for; this is not the sort of study on which to embark if there has been a recent bereavement in the class.

While there should be no difficulty in provoking discussion on this topic, if it concentrates on the question whether or not there really is an after-life it can only advance towards a built-in stalemate. The sort of approach suggested here is expected to occupy at the very least three lessons, but with all the potential it could run for as much as half a term. To treat the subject in no more than one lesson, as is sometimes done, is a frivolous approach and a waste of potential pupil interest.

As to the repressing of death as a subject of adult conversation, this can be a study in itself with older children, without sinking into morbidity; again presentation is essential. Readers who feel that any talk on death is morbid should ask why they think that. After all, death is a fact of life.

CHAPTER NINE

The Nightmare Theologick

THEN I SAW A NEW BED AND A new bedside table; for the first bed and the first bedside table had passed away, and the carpet was no more. And I saw the eminent professor, prepared as an academic robed for graduation procession, and I heard a great voice from the wardrobe saying:

'Behold, school teaching on the life of Christ is in a mess – I make all things new.'

Out of the wardrobe clambered two sorry-looking figures. They both looked biblical, if you can look biblical, but rather shop-soiled. The eminent professor stepped forward to introduce them.

'These,' he said, 'are adult versions of Jesus that children encounter. And they are very dubious, extremely dubious.' He glared through his pince-nez and moved towards one, who cowered back.

'This chap' – clouting him on the back – 'is the Jesus of the primary schools and little children's books. Just look at him.' I must admit that he looked a sorry sight. Tall, thin, pale, with a long white robe, dreamily poetic.

'They think he wandered round Galilee,' began the professor in a more hectoring tone, 'uttering philosophical remarks, kissing babies, patting old women on the head, claiming to be Son of God, being rejected and killed. Too goody-goody. Quite unbiblical, as even a glance at the New Testament will show. An impostor. Little wonder

he makes some children sceptical about the very existence of
Jesus.'

The dejected figure shrugged his shoulders slightly, with a long-
suffering air.

'And this one' – the professor stepped towards the second figure –
'Look at him!' He looked more uncouth than the first. Straggly, greasy
hair, stubble, an unkempt beard, a resentful face, a dirty robe.

'This,' resumed the professor, 'is another adult version. Here we have
the revolutionary out-to-turn-society-upside-down, world's-first-
socialist Jesus. He gives some Christians an excuse for political, even
military extremism.' They glowered at each other, but it was the
professor who got the better glower and continued: 'He, too, is a
creature of fiction. I don't find you, sir, in my New Testament.' The
other leered sullenly, but the professor turned upon both figures saying,
'You are illusions, ILLUSIONS (he shouted). Be gone!' The two un-
fortunates retreated hastily into the wardrobe.

The professor bestowed an unctuous smile upon the bedroom in
general, as if very pleased that he had disposed of the interruption to
his lecture so effectively.

'Now you see,' he went on, 'that when we all think about Jesus we
tend to read back into him the ideals and character we admire. No one
is immune from this tendency (modest cough), not even myself. Even
in the nineteenth century German scholars (he winked) did this in their
quest for the real, historical Jesus as they tried to construct a biography
of his life, but Schweitzer put them right by exposing this tendency to
create their own Jesus. Only (he winked again) Schweitzer went on to
create his own Jesus too! So we must all come to terms with our tendency to read things back or uncritically to accept other people's versions – children in secondary schools must be helped to do this.'

He paused to polish his pince-nez and turning to the wardrobe said:
'You can come out now.'

There emerged an elderly man in a suit, with white hair and carrying
a pile of scholarly books.

'This man,' said the professor proudly, 'is a theological scholar.'

The scholar bowed. Meanwhile from the wardrobe came three
removal men pushing a grand piano and a fourth carrying the stool.
The scholar sat at the piano and the removal men went back into the
wardrobe.

'And now,' said the scholar, 'I should like to play you a little number, lyrics by me set to a melody by Haydn called "Austria".' So to 'Austria' he played and sang:

> Lots and lots of German scholars
> Tried to trace the life of Christ;
> Texts and tomes and scripts they follers
> But in fact with luck they diced;
> For each picture they arrived at
> Varied from the one next door:
> Just as if they had connived at
> Fiction, fancy, myth galore.
>
> Now in modern times we're better –
> So we say and so we think;
> But our efforts are much wetter,
> In the same mistakes we sink.
> Yet again we fail to see
> The nature of New Testament:
> Christ through eyes of others viewed there
> We must first see what *they* meant.

I seemed to hear the echoes of a chorus, deep in the wardrobe, singing the last line again, but the scholar turned.

'Brings a tear to me eye, old boy,' said the scholar. 'They aren't writing music like that any more. Look at the message. We've got to see that by the very nature of the New Testament documents there's no easy life of Christ. The gospels are products of the early church, written to fulfil their interests and needs, not to provide us with a *Woman's Own* biography about Jesus' childhood, education, hobbies and love life.'

As the piano dissolved into the dressing table he continued:

'Maybe we get our impressions from a literal reading of stained-glass windows, when really they're trying to say something more subtle than what Jesus looked like, or perhaps our impressions come from seeing too many serene crucifixes in churches. But this is only the negative side of the issue.'

And taking a bow he shuffled off out of the bedroom and down the stairs. Meanwhile from the wardrobe was coming a large crowd of people: artists, sculptors, musicians, authors, ordinary folk, all carrying signs of their trade or vocation and wearing all sorts of period costumes from togas to modern dress. The professor somehow got lost in the crowd which was jostling and pushing, but finally fighting his way to the front he announced with an air of propriety:

'Now this is the other side of the coin. Although we can't see Jesus as he was, what we might call "the figure of Jesus" has fascinated and influenced people in all walks of life for centuries: artists, writers, political and religious leaders. The figure of Jesus has captured men's minds and stamped itself almost indelibly on civilization. Children, too, find this figure compelling.'

As the crowd receded into the pattern on the curtains he continued:

'So there is another side to this problem of "Who was Jesus?". To evade the problem with children is to dodge your responsibility to deal with one of the most important men in history. To solve the problem for them is to remove their right to think and ponder and eventually decide for themselves.' He paused and smiled. 'I suppose you'll be wanting to know how to proceed.'

Voices could be heard on the stairs, getting louder and approaching the bedroom. The landing light came on and, apparently unaware of the professor and the bedroom, two men walked in deep in conversation.

'Yes,' said one, 'I like that approach to the topic in the classroom.'

'Well,' said the other, 'it brings home to children the subjectivity of their assessment of historical figures in such a way that they grasp the point, without having to go into all sorts of abstract terms like "subjectivity", Donald.'

'They're RE teachers,' hissed the professor in a loud stage whisper.

'I see,' said Donald, unaware of his audience, 'so you'd start by asking them to write down in a couple of sentences the answer to the question "Who was Hitler?".'

'Exactly,' said the other, 'and you'd get as many answers as there were children. Some might write about an evil genius who tried to conquer the world, others about a thwarted young man looking for vengeance with the Jews as scapegoat, others about him seizing power at exactly the right time economically – being favoured by circumstances and so on. Then you'd simply get some of these statements read out to the whole class. They'd see for themselves how widely we differ in our assessment of people.'

'But,' said Donald as they paced up and down the bedroom, 'where do you go from there, Terence?'

'Well,' said Terence, 'you introduce the Jesus problem by setting them exactly the same exercise with the question "Who was Jesus?".'

There'll be a similar range of answers and that gives you the material for Stage Two.'

D: Which is?

T: You show again how we all vary in our assessment of people, and then look in detail at some of the answers to see the pictures they've presented. The usual adult ones come through, the meek and mild, gentle Jesus and so on.

D: You could then by work-sheets compare these with biblical pictures. . . .

T: In particular such things as the overthrowing of the money-changers' tables, the attack on the Pharisees, the rebuke to Peter – which all call in question the meek and mild Jesus. . . .

D: The revolutionary Jesus could be compared with favourable and unfavourable textual evidence in the same way. . . .

T: As could the various other pictures.

D: I like that idea. It guarantees a more informed discussion and could lead into an analysis of where the class members think they derived their picture from: Sunday Schools, stained glass windows and other sources. But when you've challenged or smashed these pictures by confronting them with textual evidence what do you think could replace it, without substituting your own personal picture?

T: That *is* a danger of this sort of iconoclastic approach, I must admit. I think it can be met by providing very careful follow-up work: the nature of gospels, their aims and origin, how their writers saw Jesus, perhaps compare the Jesus of Matthew and Luke's gospels. Then you would have to go on to examine terms the early Christians used to describe Jesus. You know how vital it is that the 'right' questions are asked of the gospel material, not questions they were simply never intended to answer.

D: Yet look at how many children are still taught in RE that the gospels are biographies of Jesus.

T: A very dangerous over-simplification.

D: Absolutely.

T: I would want to go further than text discussion to redress the negative part of the exercise. Slides, records, discussion could be used to illustrate the impact of the 'figure of Jesus' through the ages.

D: You could then explore how harmful, if harmful at all, they think the popular pictures of Jesus are and whether they can be avoided. Ask them what they would tell their children about Jesus.

T: Certainly it's the right framework within which to set discussion, backed up as we've said with careful information-finding and necessary academic background.

D: I couldn't agree more. So much discussion asks children to talk out of their heads and then is surprised to find it produces sheer prejudice or ignorance.

T: Well, I think this topic would have to run for several weeks, at a couple of periods per week, to be at all worthwhile, perhaps for up to half a term.

D: I do feel that it should be tackled, though, because otherwise children may live with their uncritically inherited picture of Jesus for ever.

They seemed to be moving inevitably towards the wardrobe.

T: By the way, I've been meaning to pick your brains on new ideas for ROSLA RE. . . .

And they were gone.

The professor reappeared from one of the darker corners of the room, putting on his mortar-board and gathering up his books and papers.

'I don't want to detain you much longer,' he said, 'because you'll be wanting to wake up.'

But there was a scuffling in the wardrobe, and finally out ran a fat man with sandwich boards on which were written various hints about teaching the life of Jesus. He stood panting.

'Oh, yes,' said the professor, 'I'll leave you further notes to help you read up this topic.'

The fat man mopped his brow and ran back while the professor, having gathered together his remaining books stood quite still, as if listening for something. Sure enough a clomping could be heard on the stairs and into the bedroom came a large yellow horse.

'I'm so glad he found the right house,' said the professor, as the horse munched the coverlet, 'he's the fifth horse of the Apocalypse, you know, but he wasn't very well on "the day" so they didn't take him out. They lend him to me when I'm on nights.' The horse having mistaken a tin of talcum powder for a carrot was cheerfully scrunching it up.

'Cheerio,' called the professor, mounting, 'I bet you could almost write a book about all the things you've seen during the night.' And they cantered down the stairs and off into the morning.

Further help for the teacher

Suggested teacher's aim

To examine critically the common assumptions about the personality and character of Jesus and to encourage children to ask the question 'Who was Jesus?' for themselves.

Academic background for the teacher

(*a*) *Introductory*

D. E. Nineham, *Saint Mark*, Penguin 1963, esp. pp. 11–52; H. A. Guy, *The Gospel of Mark*, Macmillan 1968, esp. pp. 1–43.

See references in Bible dictionaries and standard works to the theme of the Messianic secret in Mark's gospel. Mark uses this idea to develop this picture of the mystery of Jesus by suggesting that Jesus deliberately kept his true identity secret until his trial (14.62), preferring the term 'Son of Man' to any explicit claim to divinity. Thus the earliest gospel provides no support at all for the picture of a Jesus rejected because of his claims to divinity.

(*b*) *Advanced*

A. O. Dyson, *Who is Jesus Christ?*, SCM Press 1969; J. Reumann, *Jesus in the Church's Gospels*, SPCK 1970; H. Riesenfeld, *The Gospel Tradition*, Blackwell 1968, esp. pp. 1–110; S. W. Sykes and J. P. Clayton (eds.), *Christian Faith and History*, CUP 1972, esp. essays 6, 8, 10–12; G. A. Wells, *The Jesus of the Early Christians*, Pemberton 1971.

Useful material for the classroom

Commercially this is not a well-supported area of RE and consequently most materials in terms of worksheets and exercises must be self-produced. One obvious area in preparation must be a listing of pericopae which clash sharply with conventional views of Jesus, e.g. his anger: Mark 3.5; 8.33; 9.19; 10.14; 11.15; Matt. 10.15; 11.20–24; 23. 25, 31–36.

On the question of the Messianic secret read the commentators such as Nineham on passages like Mark 3.12; 8.12; 14.62 and Matt. 27.11.

For a glimpse of the figure of Jesus in primitive preaching read up *Kerygma* in the standard works and refer children to passages such as Acts 2.22–24, which may be a summary of primitive preaching on the subject.

The whole question of our picture of Jesus can be set in the context of two neglected facts: he was non-European and Jewish. Children need to be reminded of this, and the passages which emphasize his Jewishness (e.g. Matt. 5.20; 10.5).

Visually, of course, different views of Jesus can be very well demonstrated from art and sculpture down the ages. It pays to build up a personal collection of postcards and pictures cut out from magazines, etc., as a basis for making your own posters. Properly mounted and clearly labelled posters make far more impact than un-backed cards or messy mounting. Collecting your own material has another advantage – you *can* take it with you when you go!

The sort of material you can use includes photographs of the Sutherland tapestry at Coventry, the Grünewald Isenheim altarpiece; pieces by Blake, El Greco, Rubens; icons, mosaics and wall paintings. Visual Publications (197 Kensington High Street, London W8) have produced a series of filmstrips with commentary on the life of Christ seen through the eyes of the artist (1970). Although one would not want to show the whole of these – far too many teachers show whole filmstrips where they wouldn't dream of slogging through whole textbooks from cover to cover – clips from these filmstrips can be useful in class.

Since most parish churches will contain depictions of Jesus, teaching schemes on this topic would expect to draw on whatever material was near at hand for the children to observe themselves. The pop scene is 'near' to children and contemporary depictions from there are worth analysis.

For a view of Jesus from outside Christian tradition see E. G. Parrinder, *Jesus in the Qu'ran*, Faber 1965; A. H. Silver, *Where Judaism differed*, Collier-Macmillan 1956.

For a children's book on this angle see D. Stacey, *The Man from Nazareth*, REP 1969. There are some useful discussion questions on pp. 139ff. The text may be more helpful to you than the class.

In preparing the discussion aspects of this topic plan the phrasing of the questions in advance. Not only does this spare you from bungling around with vague questions or abstracts in the lesson itself – it also ensures ease of revision and re-preparation on your part when you come to teach the topic again. The non-specialist would do well to buy for his own use Edwin Cox, *This Elusive Jesus*, Marshalls Educational 1975, which is devoted entirely to the problems of gospel teaching.

CHAPTER TEN

Jailbreak at Creaking Creek

SHERIFF HORATIO HIGGINS SUCKED HIS cheroot with deep satisfaction and spat pleasurably on the floor in the way that all good lawmen do. Taking his legs off the desk – his spurs had tangled with the bills in the Pending tray – he sat up with a new vigour and contentment.

'Wait till I tell Wyatt about this,' he thought, 'he'll be green with envy.' He blew a couple of smoke rings towards the ceiling, and continued to muse. 'Fancy me capturing Black Jack, and him the most wanted outlaw in the West, locked up in the jail of li'l ol' Creaking Creek.'

He fingered the cell key lovingly and polished his badge on his braces. His mind lingered on the showdown the night before on the main street: the empty sidewalks, the flickering oil lamps, the saloon piano silenced, eyes at the windows, the silence of the night, and at the far end of the street the massive figure of Black Jack, itching to draw his six-shooter.

'Good job I slugged him from behind,' thought Horatio. But he was interrupted by the arrival in his office of his deputy, Billy the Goat.

'Hi,' drawled Horatio, 'I gotten us a real prize locked up in there.' He nodded in the direction of the cells.

'Sure,' said Billy, 'I heard about it from a Fargo driver.'

'Yeah.'

'Yeah.'

'Sure.'

'Sure.'

'Wanna take a look at him?'

'Yeah.'

'Oh yeah?'

'Yeah.'

'Goldarned conversation conventions,' thought Horatio, 'but a man has to do what a man has to do. . . .' He picked up the keys and led the way proudly to the cells, opening first the locked door into the corridor that led to the cell block.

'I'll go first,' he said, 'Black Jack sure is a mean man, but he makes a prize buzzard in a cage.' He opened the double lock on the cell door, then the door itself – and opened his mouth almost as wide. The cell was deserted. There was no sign of Black Jack. The Sheriff was speechless. But his deputy with all the agility of any western hero grasped the situation immediately.

'He ain't here,' he said, 'sure ain't.'

The cell was certainly empty. No sign of how the escape could have been made either: the bars on the window were undisturbed, and Horatio held in his hand the only keys to the door. Outside on the sidewalk could be heard the shrill giggle of Dolores from the Silver Dime Saloon. But inside the two men stood in deep and perplexed silence.

Let us leave them there, for the moment, and invite the reader to join us as we ponder their situation, and the situation of the RE teacher dealing with so-called miracles – 'so-called' because the term itself conjures up a certain unhelpful impression and anyway occurs only rarely in the New Testament. Strange as it may seem, the situation at Creaking Creek as we look at it has a lot in common with the NT miracles as we may look at them with children:

(*a*) There is little data on which to theorize. One would like to know so much more, but few of the NT accounts supply more than the minimal information. There are exceptions such as the Legion incident, or that involving the epileptic boy, but even in these cases there is nothing approaching detail in the accounts. Yet despite this we, like Horatio and Billy, are challenged to come to terms with these incidents.

(*b*) Just as those reading of the dilemma of the two lawmen have been deprived of the possibility of reading it in the context of a whole novel, which would enable the writer's aims to be more clearly seen, and hence thrown light on this one incident, so those who discuss miracles with children too readily tear them from their context, thus depriving children of the chance to see why, for example, Mark felt

these were important and how he used them in his total gospel structure. Or again children are sometimes deprived of the necessary Old
Testament background to the understanding of an account.

(c) You could produce broadly the same theories if you were writing
the saga of Creaking Creek as you can when dealing with miracles,
namely:

1. *The supernatural intervention theory.* In our story Black Jack would
have been spirited away and the mystery would remain. In NT terms
God would intervene in a way not humanly understood in order to
perform his will, using processes not known to science.

2. *The rationalist theory.* In this case one would start by assuming that
all events, however odd, are capable of rational explanation. It seems
unlikely that Black Jack could have tunnelled out (since the account
suggests an undisturbed room), so an explanation based on the locks
having been picked seems preferable. With NT miracles you would
suggest psychosomatic roots of illness, or in 'nature miracles' such as
the stilling of the storm you might argue that the wind was becalmed
just as Jesus was saying to the disciples 'Be still' and the whole thing was
misunderstood.

3. *The sceptical theory.* The mystery of Creaking Creek can't be
solved as it stands. Something must be false. Horatio and Billy must be
'in' on it for their own purposes and rigged it. Transposed to the NT
situation this means that the gospel writers rigged it and their accounts
must be rejected. Although few if any modern scholars would approach
the miracles from this point of view, some modern children certainly
would, as any RE teacher quickly finds out. More often than not they
are suffering from an overdose of Bible in the primary school, where
sometimes insensitive, misguided, evangelical or plain ignorant teachers
have lifted biblical material uncritically and in so doing sowed the seeds
of uncritical rejection in the secondary school.

We suggest that, generally speaking, all these approaches are un-
profitable because they take insufficient account of the material in its
context; they argue from single accounts, which taken singly provide
insufficient data; as theories they reflect more of the teacher's or children's own presuppositions, failing to deal with the material as 'objec-
tively' as their proponents imagine. We recommend an approach,
therefore, based on these principles:

1. *Clarity of definition.* The question of definition must be discussed fully. For example, someone who holds that a miracle is that which never happens is committed by definition to a set conclusion in any examination of evidence. The teacher can offer various definitions such as Augustine's often-quoted view that a miracle is not contrary to nature but to what is known of nature. If a miracle can be explained away, does it cease to be a miracle? What words does the NT prefer ('Mighty acts', 'signs' etc.)? Why? Were they really supposed to prove anything? Is a miracle that which causes us to wonder? Was the converted alcoholic right when he claimed to have witnessed a miracle because in his house beer had turned into furniture? If 'God acting' is itself a miracle, must it inevitably defy scientific analysis? Or does God not intervene to break laws he has created? These are some of the questions that must be asked. So much enquiry is stunted by lack of clarity of definition and the first aim in the classroom must be to rectify this. .

2. *The need to see the miracles against their contemporary background.* The Bible miracles must be set in the context of the ancient world, a world of wonder-workers, a world where 'pagans' were held to perform miracles. This means thinking back into an era where the miraculous was accepted and expected. Even Jesus' opponents who claimed that he was devil-possessed did not dispute that he healed people – they could only impugn the source of his power. Along with this, of course, goes the need to see the miracles against the gospel background and in the context of the aims of their writers.

3. *The miracles must be seen in the light of subsequent cases in Christian tradition and in other religions.* Spiritual healing continues. Lourdes flourishes. Eastern mystics appear to defy pain – and sometimes gravity. Alleged cases of paranormal phenomena are always cropping up in the media. Principalities and powers have not been banished, from popular thinking at any rate. The aim of an excursus such as this into a wider field is not to prove or disprove anything. Rather it is to examine similarities and differences in this whole series of phenomena, to study several really well-documented cases, and perhaps to question the enormous physical/materialist/empirical emphasis on proof in contemporary western culture. Other avenues will inevitably open – the question of the power (and hence nature) of prayer, the nature of spirit and so on.

It is important for children and adults to see that the questions must be asked in the right order. 'Did miracles happen?' is certainly not the first. Definition, sources, evidence, alternative hypotheses must all be examined beforehand. For whatever stumbling block these events have become for modern man they did not preoccupy the ancients to the same extent. We too must be patient in our thinking about this complex issue; otherwise teachers run the risk that they will simply succeed in creating confusion and perpetuating prejudice.

Billy scratched his head.

'So where do we go from here? Wanted posters on every tree? A posse in search of the varmint?'

'Steady on, partner,' said Horatio, 'ain't no call to go chargin' about like an unbroke stallion.' They walked out of the cell and sat down in the office, helping themselves to a coffee and spitting the ritual bit of cheroot in the direction of the fire bucket. 'We gotta go by the rules,' he continued, spurs again in the Pending tray, 'list the possibilities, wire the Pinkerton Agency to supply us with a list of details o' sim'lar events. Then we gotta chew over the evidence we got.' They paused as a dude walked by on the sidewalk.

'Can't we just blame it on Injuns?' asked Billy.

'Nope. It's too goldarned complex to be that simple. Why, the whole West might be lookin' to us to set an example in terms o' proper investigation methods.'

Silence.

'So how ya gonna tackle it, Horatio?'

Silence.

'I'm gonna get me a good bit o' bedside readin'.'

Silence.

'What'll ya do till then?'

The stage coach from Dodge City clattered in and drew up opposite. Horatio watched dreamily as the stage unloaded, the driver gently hurling the cases marked 'Fragile' to the floor. The passengers dispersed. The horses were untethered and led away to be stabled.

'What'll ya do till then?' said Billy again. Horatio stood up slowly and stretched himself. He yawned, then ambled towards the door, putting on his gunbelt and hat.

'I'm gonna do what all good cowboys do,' he said, 'so put the record on.'

Billy wound the gramophone and soon the strains of 'Home on the Range' could be heard. Horatio mounted his horse and to the sound of the theme music rode off down the mainstreet towards a caption marked

THE END

Further help for the teacher

Suggested teacher's aim
To examine with children (*a*) the problem of definition involved; (*b*) specific examples, in their context, and to teach some understanding of the NT material.

Academic background for the teacher
(*a*) *Introductory*
R. H. Fuller, *Interpreting the Miracles*, SCM Press 1963; Alan Richardson, *The Miracle Stories of the Gospels*, SCM Press, 1941.

(*b*) *For further study*
C. S. Lewis, *Miracles – A Preliminary Study*, Bles 1947, Fontana 1960; C. Morris, *The Hammer of the Lord*, Epworth 1973, pp. 125–134, contains a brief but lively discussion of one possible view in contemporary Christianity; C. F. D. Moule, *Miracles*, Mowbrays 1965; I. T. Ramsey (et al.), *The Miracles and the Resurrection*, SPCK 1964; also L. Rose, *Faith Healing*, Gollancz 1968, revised Penguin 1971, and for an opposing point of view, C. Woodard, *A Doctor Heals by Faith*, Parrish 1953; L. D. Weatherhead, *Psychology, Religion and Healing*, Hodder 1963.

For a discussion of the philosophical issues involved see A. C. MacIntyre, *Difficulties in Christian Belief*, SCM Press 1959, ch. 5.

For useful material on the attitudes to this question at a different point in Christian tradition see K. Thomas, *Religion and the Decline of Magic*, esp. chapters 7–9, Penguin University Books 1973: this is a study of popular beliefs in the sixteenth and seventeenth centuries in England.

Useful material for the classroom
Unfortunately many producers of commercial material have shied away from what they have seen as a very difficult topic, and much of

the material that does exist is very confessional in outlook, likely to engender more problems than it solves if used. But CSE Study Guide 3 in the *Christianity and Life* pack, Darton, Longman & Todd 1973, is useful. At the same time this is not a difficult topic on which to construct one's own resource material. Duplicated sheets in a protective folder make useful case study collections.

One way of structuring the topic

Lesson 1: Class discussion on the question of definition. This serves to open up the whole topic. As repeatedly stressed in this book, this does not mean that the teacher wanders in with some vague questions and thoughts, hoping that the class will latch on; he arrives with a carefully structured series of questions, such as those in Chapter 7, perhaps with a handout of various summary definitions for comparison. He will have planned his lesson to give the class the chance to do some written work: this not only prevents them from viewing RE as a rest but also takes into account the fact that teachers often grossly overestimate the ability of fifteen- and sixteen-year-old young people to sustain a discussion without boredom.

Lesson 2: Groups or individuals examine case studies, which again are accompanied by a written list of questions.

Lesson 3: The teacher examines with the whole group key gospel accounts in context (don't forget to consult the commentaries as you prepare).

Lesson 4: Members of the group produce and discuss material which they have been collecting since Lesson 1. This may be women's magazine accounts of paranormal phenomena, or accounts culled from library books, or accounts of TV material: here the teacher's role is to enable proper, critical discussion of these accounts and their sources, purpose, etc. to take place.

Lesson 5: The teacher draws this to a conclusion; he will have to structure this in the light of how that particular class have reacted so far. But of course conclusion must not mean, as alas it does in some schools, that at this point he browbeats the group into his way of thinking.

Note: By 'lesson' in this context we mean working through a defined section of the whole topic; this may take several periods on the school timetable. 'Lesson' here does not imply, say, thirty-five minutes curtailed by the bell.

Stage 6: Evaluation by the teacher. This should follow every lesson series ever taught, but doesn't always. The teacher must ask himself carefully and honestly:

1. Have I at any stage obtruded my views on the class?
2. Have they really finished the study knowing and thinking more than when they began?
3. Has the way in which I have structured the work developed their written skills and expression as well as oral?
   (Examine their written output carefully here.)
4. Have I done justice to the enormous amount of material and belief in this topic? (There is an allied question here: have I read sufficient to teach this adequately, and what steps am I taking to revise and extend my own grasp of the topic?)
5. Which individuals in the class have derived least from this topic? Why? Can this be remedied?
6. Which aspects of the topic obviously went down well? Can I learn from this in a way that could help me with the next topic, or if faced with this topic again?

Teachers are usually conscientious in their forward planning, but evaluation after the event is often neglected.

CHAPTER ELEVEN

Whodunnit?

OST OF US ENJOY A GOOD
thriller; we hate to be told the ending by
someone who's beaten us to it; we hate the
smugness of those who sanctimoniously assure
us that they've known since page 2 who the
murderer is; we're annoyed with ourselves when
we can't put the book down and stay up late, with
consequent irritability next morning. We like the
mystery. We like to theorize. But we like to get
there in the end. When we think of the resurrection
as a topic in the upper half of the secondary school
we can readily see that children will enjoy this debate,
chewing over theories and putting forward views of
their own. The what-happened-and-whodunnit
atmosphere surrounding the resurrection of Jesus has intrigued men
for centuries; this topic needs little sales effort to arouse interest, in a
situation of open-ended discussion, where the teacher isn't trying to
bulldoze or steer his pupils to his own conclusions.

But before we launch into how to get our amateur detectives in the
classroom involved we must sound a warning note. In an unstructured
discussion or study of this topic children – who often don't possess even
a working knowledge of NT background, textual criticism, the nature
of manuscript evidence, etc. – will produce all sorts of weird and
strange theories which they are gullible enough to talk themselves into,
since they have insufficient knowledge against which to test these
hypotheses. Sherlock Holmes always refused to theorize until he had
made a thorough survey of the information; his young disciples don't
always follow this principle!

Furthermore, the RE teacher owes it to the topic to make it very clear that what is being investigated is not merely the disappearance of a corpse (some theologians would say not *even*). The analogy of the detective, like all analogies, has limited validity. Too often RE teachers get bogged down in missing corpses leading finally to the impression that all that we are considering is the possible resuscitation of a dead man – no contact point with people now except to excite a mild scientific curiosity or a whodunnit interest.

A structured scheme of work need not lose its open-endedness, and we suggest that in order to do justice to the topic the following areas must be treated. Teachers reading this may very well wish to add more. We do not think that they can in justice to the topic add less!

(*a*) Any approach to this subject must examine the texts in question: this means some study of the accounts in the gospels and I Corinthians. It means providing background, if they don't have it, about the provenance of the gospels and the interests of the churches in which they originated. This may require a good block of quite formal teaching, because some commentary will also have to be provided on such matters as the eucharistic connection in the Emmaus story and the problem of the lost ending of Mark. Without this basis, however, all discussion will take place at a superficial level. On the other hand this doesn't have to mean the interest-killing 'take out your Bibles' approach. Why not duplicate from RSV or NEB the key passages, with important text variants? These can be stapled within card covers for future use, and with blank facing pages for pupils' notes. Time-consuming for the teacher, but helps overcome the anti-Bible reaction, and makes for easier comparison of source material.

(*b*) Discussion cannot take place without some awareness of the symbolism of language. The phrase 'Jesus lives', for example, may represent different ideas: it may mean he lives biologically; or that he lives in the sense that 'Che Guaevara' lives, in the hearts and minds of his followers; or that he lives in some other dimension of existence than those we comprehend, and so on. Children may need to be challenged to see these possibilities of meaning within one phrase. 'Rose from the dead' is another example of this sort of phrase: a literal meaning is possible, but so are others. What we are doing theologically by exploring these questions of meaning is to move children from their black-or-white literal acceptance or rejection attitude to an awareness of symbolic and mythical interpretation. This does not mean we are ruling literalism as an interpretation out of court (which would be to indoctrinate) but in honesty we must reduce its status as the sole possible interpretation.

(c) It is vital to examine presuppositions of those entering into the dialogue because if members of the group are denying persistently and consistently from the beginning the whole possibility of resurrection then obviously they can't begin to tackle this topic in a profitable way at all. The teacher's task in that situation is to put the spotlight on the presuppositions in question and discuss those. Is the basis of the denial a denial of the reality of God? Belief that the process of death cannot be reversed? A reaction against literalism? Invariably all our presuppositions are found under scrutiny to beg a whole series of questions. Thorough groundwork in tackling the bases of such presupposition may be necessary – again this can be open-ended. The aim in confronting presupposition is not to change but to make the holder aware of what he implies in his attitude and why he implies it. He himself then may or may not abandon the presupposition, and the decision is his; but he can no longer be unaware of its existence.

(d) Having stated that we ought not to encourage children to weave weird theories on this topic we must allow public debate of alternatives. If the group still produce wild hypotheses they cannot be simply dismissed peremptorily. The structure of open-ended discussion to which we are committed requires us to deal with these suggestions. The RE teacher who refuses to discuss alternatives, however painful or irritant to his own personal belief, may well produce a class of silent sceptics – we use sceptic in the sense of sceptic to his position. On the other hand, given time to argue a case children will often say that their own suggestions do not, on examination, have a convincing ring.

Some of the alternatives are as old as Christianity itself: the disciples stole the body; Jesus was in deep coma and revived; hysterical women went to the wrong tomb; some substitute was crucified in Jesus' stead, etc. Some alternatives reflect sensationalism in the press and by renegade scholars, e.g. Jesus was an astronaut from an alien planet, possessed of superior powers, able to heal people and resurrect himself. Many children in this SF age find all this quite acceptable, especially if it's been 'on telly'; the RE teacher who gets himself steamed up about it merely illustrates his own prejudices. His real role is not to attack, but to provide a critique of all these views. Moreover it is interesting to note that nearly all these alternative explanations concentrate on the empty tomb

and are built around that. In the interests of presenting a balanced picture it is worth bringing to the attention of the class the fact that Paul,
although writing well before the gospels, places no emphasis on the
tomb, empty or otherwise. He stresses the 'resurrection experience' of
other Christians and of himself. He holds that this experience streng-
thens their faith and witness, and is uninterested in graveyard
disappearances (cf. I Cor. 9.1f.; 12.27; 15.4 in the context of
15.35ff.).

In providing a critique of alternatives the teacher will want to question them, as well as letting them question Christian tradition. He will
want to ask, for example, whether it is likely that a substitute could
have been crucified in Jesus' place. At what point could the switch be
made? When the teacher turns to examine Christian tradition he will
pose pros and cons: is the continuation of Christianity a demonstration
that in some sense Jesus lives? But then how would the post-resurrection
appearances fit into such a view? . . .

The role of the RE teacher is to create a situation in which informed
discussion can take place. He must provide a critique of the various
views put forward, and of the biblical evidence. He may yet have to
come to terms with the fact that in an absolute sense no one can
know for certain what happened on that far-away Sunday morning
and the days following; in that sense one cannot prove or disprove
anything. On the other hand people, having considered possibilities
and probabilities, have accepted that 'the Lord is risen' (with varying
degrees of interpretation) and claim this is confirmed in the life of the
church and in personal experience. The RE teacher is not like a secular
evangelist to try to force his children to decide for or against *now*,
today. He is the 'midwife' for a discussion which may be of help to
them when they are ready to come to terms with this most basic of
Christian beliefs.

Further help for the teacher

Suggested teacher's aim
To consider the various interpretations of the resurrection of Jesus, at
various stages in the history of Christianity, and to stimulate the children
to further thought on the topic.

Academic background for the teacher

(*a*) *Introductory*

R. P. C. Hanson (ed.), *Difficulties for Christian Belief*, Macmillan 1967, ch. 3; T. E. Jessop, *An Introduction to Christian Doctrine*, Nelson 1960, ch. 7; V. Taylor, *The Formation of the Gospel Tradition*, Macmillan 1935, ch. 3.

Most important, of course, by way of introduction are the relevant passages in the commentaries.

(*b*) *Advanced*

R. H. Fuller, *The Formation of the Resurrection Narratives*, SPCK 1971; C. F. Evans, *Resurrection and New Testament*, SCM Press 1970; R. Bultmann and others, *Life and Death* (Bible Key Words), A. & C. Black 1965; I. T. Ramsey, *The Miracles and the Resurrection*, SPCK 1965.

For classroom use

For older pupils, or for ideas on presentation for the teacher, C. Chapman, *Christianity on Trial*, Lion 1974, Vol. 3, is attractively presented and reasonably priced. Also for older pupils there is a short section in P. Miller and K. Pound, *Creeds and Controversies*, EUP 1969, ch. 24, again a book which is very useful as an ideas book for the teacher, even if not adopted as a class text. Another 'ideas book', J. Tooke and K. Russell, *Projects in Religious Education*, Batsford 1974, devotes pp. 20–27 to the death (but not resurrection) of Jesus. As suggested in Chapter 11 itself, older children should certainly come to grips with the biblical accounts for themselves, but with commentary help supplied either by the teacher or from the easier commentaries such as the SCM Press Torch series.

Younger secondary children, and less able ones, derive very little from being plunged into detailed discussion on this question. If you are dealing with aspects of the life of Jesus at first or second year level it is sufficient to stress that the early Christians believed that Jesus was alive and that modern Christians believe that in some sense this is still true today. They were changed and excited by what they felt to be his presence. . . . This avoids discussing at an intellectual level they have not reached yet (viva Saint Piaget, beloved of educationalists!) and gives them something which does not have to be untaught higher up the school. Moreover it is perfectly acceptable to Jews, atheists, Moslems, humanists and all that this is how the early Christians interpreted their experience. Whether they were right to do so is the upper school discussion question.

CHAPTER TWELVE

The Mything Link

ONCE, O WELL-BELOVED, WHEN THE world was young and the sweet waters sang in the fountains of Eldarol, there came a day when the gods grew bored.

'What's the time?' said Nog to Clog.

'A quarter to three.'

'More than an hour till nectar time! How these afternoons drag! We've done everything there is to do. We've run in the golden fields of Weldar, swum in the silver pool of Pelanin; we've slept under the scented apple blossom in the orchards of Nisboth, and we can't play tiddlywinks because you fed all the counters to the goldfish. Isn't there *anything* else we can do?'

'I know!' exclaimed Clog. 'Let's invent a new creature: a mystery-creature, unlike any creature ever invented before. And we'll ask all the other gods to help too.'

Nog thought this was a good idea, so they went first to Prog who was sunning himself in a greenhouse, and then to the two sisters Toga and Yoga who weren't. Eventually they had gathered together all the gods, and they sat together under the boughs of the cedar tree beside the laughing brook that flows into the land of men. Only Geran was not invited, and he was too old and deaf to enjoy their sport.

There, under the cedar tree, the gods talked and argued. Each insisted that the mystery-creature should do him credit, and each gave him a fine attribute. Nog gave him the gift of poetry; Clog gave him the gift of story-telling; Prog gave spiritual vision; Toga gave the power to conjure up deep-seated images from the minds of men; Yoga gave the gift of knowledge. Og himself gave the power of scientific analysis, deduction and explanation.

When the mystery-creature was complete it stood before the gods, sprightly and bewitching, yet tender and thoughtful; very young and yet very old.

'We must give it a name,' said Toga. But the gods could not agree on a name. Some said one thing, some said another. So they took it to Geran, and Prog shouted down his ear-trumpet, 'We want you to suggest a name for this; it's a mystery-creature.'

'It's a what?' asked Geran, who had not quite heard.

'A mystery-creature!'

'A myth?'

'That's it!' shouted all the gods. 'We'll call it a Myth!'

The Myth lived happily in the Land of Eldarol for some months while the gods enjoyed their new toy. But in time they grew bored again, and the Myth began to yearn for adventure. One afternoon while the gods were taking their siesta he tied together some bundles of papyrus reed and made for himself a small raft. He launched out into the laughing brook, and was carried away and away, till he drifted down into the land of men.

In the early days of his sojourn with men the Myth found he was a welcome visitor. Many were the evenings when men sat round a fire and called upon him to tell his stories. They delighted in the gifts which the gods had bestowed upon him, and sometimes they even turned his stories into plays and rituals. So deeply did his stories move them that they came to believe that if he ever died the world would die with him. And wherever men trod the earth, the Myth was guest of honour.

But their favour did not last for ever, for men grew arrogant with the knowledge and power which the Myth had given them, and they made a plot to imprison the Myth. They tied him up and wrote him down on tablets of clay, and set children to copy him out in schoolrooms for year after year. The Myth grew stiff and the sparkle left his eyes. And when in later years he was written down in a book, people looked at him and thought how plain he was.

'Just history,' they would say, and pass on.

For long years the Myth lay bound in the dungeons of the Bible, and even his old clay tablets were buried deep in the earth. He was old and weak and his beard was long. Kings forgot him, and princes dismissed him as a foolish old thing, until at last the day came when someone found some of the old tablets on which he had been written down. Curious, men sought him out once more, and when they looked more closely at him they saw not a foolish old thing, but a stately creature of wide experience and of wisdom. Then the prison doors were unbarred, the chains were broken and the Myth went free. There was great rejoicing. In time he regained something of his former youth, and men everywhere turned their thoughts to their ancestors and knew in their hearts how much they owed to the Myth.

And do you know, O well-beloved, that to this day the Myth can still be seen wandering the streets and tapping on doors? Should he ever come to your door, do not turn him away. No – ask him in, welcome him to your fireside, and press a warming drink into his hands; and bring in your friends to listen to his story. For remember, he is the mystery-creature of the gods.

What the teacher must bear in mind is that to children the word 'myth' means at best a fairy-tale, or at worst a lie. Our task is to educate pupils towards a more mature appreciation of the nature of myth. We should certainly not try to prove that the myths of the Bible are true, either literally or in any other way. What we must do is to suggest that myths are serious statements which require serious consideration.

One way of doing this is to present myth as a form of primitive scientific explanation which also embodies a religious value judgment. The best-known example of a biblical myth, the Priestly creation story of Genesis 1.1–2.3, lends itself well to this approach, although others do also. The analysis which follows is not intended as a lesson-scheme for teaching the topic of creation (which is very much wider). It is simply to show one possible 'way in' to a mythical text.

1. *The Priestly creation story as scientific statement.* To appreciate the statement being made one must examine the picture of the universe which is presupposed by the myth. This picture is that the world is surrounded by water. Why should the ancient Hebrews, among others, have thought this? Presumably because rain falls from the sky and wells up in springs and seas from beneath the earth. In addition both sky and sea look blue. Given the limits of ancient science the deduction is a reasonable one.

What the creation story does, scientifically, is to put forward a hypothesis concerning the sequence of events which produced the present state of the world and universe. It is working within the limits. According to the hypothesis a small area is separated off in the middle of the waters by a hard layer ('firmament'), presumably in the shape of a dome; then the waters are evacuated from under it (the waters are 'gathered together'). The hollow space then forms the area between land, now inserted, and sky (the dome), and by stages it is peopled with vegetation, heavenly bodies, animals and men.

This way of viewing the creation story is easily presented to younger children through a series of simple diagrams illustrating the four or five logical steps in the story. Incidentally, the 'seven days' bear no resemblance to these logical, scientific stages and are a didactic feature imposed on the story by Priestly editors. Older children may be able to arrive at this view by themselves if given careful guidance. A work-card with text and suitable guiding questions would be appropriate provided – as always with work-cards – that the matter received adequate class discussion as well.

2. *The Priestly creation story as religious statement.* Not every feature of the myth can be accounted for as a product of scientific explanation. What other elements are there, and what religious views do they express? Among others there are:

(*a*) An explanation why the sabbath should be observed. This is what the seven-day scheme leads up to. So here the myth is being used to support an established custom. An earlier and different reason for observing the sabbath is given in Deuteronomy 5.14f.

(*b*) A description of the status and role of man. Man is created last, and is viewed as the pinnacle of creation. He is called the 'image of God'. This phrase is difficult to interpret, but it probably recalls the way in which conquering kings used to set up their statues to remind vassal states of their sovereignty. If so, the term does not describe either the physical appearance or spiritual character of man, but his function.

(*c*) Above all, a judgment on the purpose of the world. The world is here because God wants it to be. To appreciate that this really is a feature separable from the scientific statement, and not just another bit of (automatically outmoded) science, one should compare the Genesis myth with other Near Eastern myths of creation. Many of the same elements appear and sometimes the same picture is in the background. But the judgment is different: creation is haphazard or accidental or a natural outcome of the forces of nature. It is important to make these comparisons in the classroom, so that children can see that myth is a genuine and widespread phenomenon rather than a 'cover up' category invented to save the Bible from disgrace. Creation-myths, particularly,[1] lend themselves to colourful presentation on the blackboard.

This sort of presentation, distinguishing between explanation and evaluation, can be applied to most myths and especially to those which, like the biblical myths, have been adapted by ancient writers to theological uses. The old cliché that 'science' answers the question 'How?' while the Bible answers the question 'Why?' is incorrect. Biblical myths do both. How far they are still both acceptable is a matter which can be discussed in class, but on which pupils must make up their own minds. Our job is to open their eyes to the complexity, subtlety and startling sanity of these myths. They are a responsible form of tradition, and must be treated responsibly.

Further help for the teacher

Suggested teacher's aim
To enable children to understand the nature of myth and its role in ancient and modern society.

Academic background for the teacher
(a) *Introductory*
There are problems here, because many of the books on myth are very highly specialized and rather unreadable. Moreover, because of the tendency now to equate the terms 'myth' and 'fiction' in popular thinking we may find it very hard to approach this subject at a more technical level. So, granted that these introductory books may not be 'easy' we suggest:

The New Encyclopaedia of Mythology, Hamlyn 1959; G. S. Kirk, *Myth*, CUP 1970; T. Fawcett, *The Symbolic Language of Religion*, SCM Press 1970; *Folklore, myths and legends of Britain*, Reader's Digest, London 1973.

(b) *Advanced*
H. Frankfort (et al.), *Before Philosophy*, Penguin 1949; R. Graves, *The*

1. See further T. Copley and D. Easton, *What they never told you about RE*, SCM Press 1974, pp. 34 and 35.

Greek Myths, Penguin 1955, revised 1960, 2 vols.; S. H. Hooke (ed.), *Myth and Ritual*, OUP 1933; S. H. Hooke (ed.), *Myth, Ritual and Kingship*, OUP 1958; S. H. Hooke, *Middle Eastern Mythology*, Penguin 1963; G. von Rad, *Genesis*, SCM Press 1961.

For creation see also: I. G. Barbour, *Issues in Science and Religion*, SCM Press 1966, esp. chs. 2, 4, 12; G. de Beer, *A Handbook on Evolution*, Natural History Museum 1970; O. Chadwick, *The Victorian Church*, A. & C. Black 1970, Vol. I, ch. 8; Vol. II, ch. 1; J. K. Crellin, *Darwin and Evolution*, Jackdaw Publications Ltd, no. 85, n.d.; W. Eichrodt, *Theology of the Old Testament*, SCM Press 1967, Vol. II, chs. 15 and 16.

Children may meet myth in the course of biblical study for CSE or 'O' level. The earlier they can understand its nature the better. So some attempt should be made at the earliest opportunity to build a study of this into the syllabus, otherwise what they take to be scepticism in adolescence – in reality an attempt to interpret myth literally – will inevitably arise as they discard as 'true' the Genesis creation stories. In fact they are simply rejecting bad teaching at an earlier, perhaps primary school, level. One textbook which tackles this topic in an attractive way for children is B. Wigley and R. Pitcher, *From Fear to Faith*, Longmans 1969. On similar lines we suggest how this can be built into a syllabus for younger, secondary children in *What they never told you about RE*, SCM Press 1974, pp. 26–30. Another book which is excellent and clear for both beginners and more advanced students is P. Grimal (ed.), *Larousse World Mythology*, Hamlyn 1973. See especially the Introduction, 'Man and Myth'.

CHAPTER THIRTEEN

Toad Hall Holidays Inc.

THE WATER LAPPED SOFTLY AGAINST the jetty as Rat and Mole brought their boat in to land. Rat jumped ashore with the line, and made it fast.

'Right ho, Mole! Now, are you sure you have the paper? Good. Then off we go.'

The Mole clambered out of the boat and adjusted the muffler round his neck. Under his arm was a folded newspaper. Spread out before them lay the spacious lawns and gardens of Toad Hall; and beyond was Toad Hall itself, ample and well-proportioned, snugly wrapped in Virginia Creeper, its leaded windows gleaming in the sun. The sight was familiar to them both, although neither had been there for some months. But suddenly Mole froze.

'Ratty! Look over there!'

Rat looked. Beside the jetty stood a large, white notice-board with a message in black letters for everyone to read.

TOAD HALL HOLIDAYS INC.
LUXURY ACCOMMODATION
MARINA, SWIMMING POOL
HEALTH FARM, SPECIAL DIETS
INDIVIDUAL ATTENTION
Phone: Toadsville 208.

'Come along,' said Rat. 'It looks as if things are worse than we feared.'

They marched, whiskers bristling, towards the front door of Toad Hall. Rat tugged at the bell-pull, and they waited. After a few moments the bolts were drawn back and the oak doors swung open. Framed in the doorway stood the portly figure of Toad, in red and gold cap and blazer, with white flannel trousers. He was brandishing a very long, very fat cigar.

'Welcome, welcome to Toad Hall!' he began, looking over their heads enraptured with his own greeting. 'This, my friends, is your lucky day! Today you embark on a new experience in holiday-making. Here at Toad Hall we offer you a holiday of distinction, a holiday of. . . .'

'Toad!' interrupted Rat. 'Stop drivelling and let us in.' Toad paused to look at his audience.

'Well, if it isn't my old friends Rat and Mole! And to think that I didn't recognize you. Ho ho! What a jape! Well, come along in, come along in.' Toad showed them through into the study.

'Sit you down, my friends. And what about a little something to warm the cockles, eh? That's the spirit! Well, well, well. Of course, you'll see some changes in the old place, what? Pretty big changes, and all. I'm in the holiday business now, you know; and in a big way, I don't mind telling you. I dare say you've heard all about Toad Hall Holidays, eh? Ha ha!'

'Yes, Toad, we have. And that's what we've come to talk to you about. Show him the paper, Mole.'

Mole unfolded the newspaper and opened it at a full-page advertisement. He read aloud, ' "Toad Hall Holidays, for better holidays in more elegant surroundings. Toad Hall will give you health, fun and friendship in a gracious, waterside environment." ' Mole looked up. 'And that's just a small sample of it. Now, what's it all about, Toad? It's time you explained what's going on.'

'I say, chaps; steady on. No need to get shirty with an old friend like Toad. Just been doing a spot of advertising, that's all. Papers, radio, television, magazines: that sort of thing.'

'That's all very well, Toad,' said Rat. 'And we don't like being hard on an old friend, but someone has to tell you. The fact is that a lot of people – powerful people, like the weasels – are saying that your advertisements are misleading. You ought to be a lot more careful. For example, where's all your luxury holiday accommodation?'

'There's a shed round the back.'

'And that's the way to have a "better" holiday?'

'Well, it's better than not having a holiday at all.'

'What about the marina and swimming-pool?'

'There's the river.'

'And the health farm?'

'Visitors can go on a grapefruit diet.'

'Tell us about the rest of the meals.'

'All visitors take the health farm holiday.'

'And what do you mean by "individual attention"?'

'We look after each person as an individual.'

'And how many individuals have come here so far?'

'Oh . . . a number. . . .'

'Exactly?'

'Well . . . one, actually.'

'I see. Individual attention! Now look, Toad. This just won't do. You're deliberately trying to mislead the public, and I can see why the weasels are angry.'

'Now hold on a minute, Ratty. You don't understand. There's nothing dishonest in any of those advertisements. It's just that if you're trying to sell something you naturally present it in the most attractive light you can. There's nothing wrong with that, now, is there?'

'But look, Toad. We agree they are not actually dishonest; but you can't deny that you're arousing expectations that you don't intend to fulfil. And what about the sorts of motives that you are appealing to? Every one of your advertisements panders to some weakness in the reader. There's one with snob-appeal, one with luxury-appeal, one with sex-appeal, one with popularity-appeal, adventure-appeal. It's all so unrealistic. What I object to,' said Rat, 'is that you are always either appealing to selfish motives or hinting at benefits which people will not really get from coming here. It's not like you, Toad, to sink to this sort of level.'

'Pooh! What a lot of nonsense you do talk, Ratty. You obviously don't understand the first thing about business. Ask anyone who really knows about these things and they'll tell you straight away: an advertisement must catch the reader's attention. You wouldn't suggest that I just put out a dull little notice in the personal column, would you?'

'But you see,' interjected Mole, 'You are using half-hidden implications to persuade people to spend money on something they would not otherwise have felt they needed.'

'I am opening up a new area of choice for the public. If they don't want to come, they needn't. And meanwhile I'm doing them a service by telling them, free, where they can get a good holiday.'

'It's true that you're opening a new area of choice,' agreed Mole. 'But aren't you also restricting the freedom of the individual to choose?'

'My dear Mole, that can't possibly be so. You're contradicting yourself.'

'I don't think so,' said Mole, shyly. 'When you work out how much to spend on advertising, don't you also calculate how many people you can count on persuading to come here? So doesn't advertising actually depend on the assumption that people will be persuaded? And if you are persuading people, aren't you also restricting their freedom to choose? What you call advertising in business has a different name in politics: propaganda, or even indoctrination.'

'Oh, I think that's going a bit too far. There are plenty of other holiday advertisements in competition with mine, so I can't be indoctrinating people. Besides, if people are gullible enough to be persuaded against their better judgment, that's their affair not mine. I just bring my holidays to their attention in as noticeable a way as I can.'

'And for whose benefit?' asked Rat. 'Yours – to make more money.'

'And theirs – to try a new holiday. And if it benefits me, what's wrong with that? I'm the one providing the service. If I make money it's because the service I provide is wanted by the public.'

The argument would have continued indefinitely, Toad growing more blustery and indignant, and Rat and Mole talking in higher and higher squeaks, if a gruff, deliberate cough had not made itself heard from the door to the study.

'Pardon me for interrupting,' grunted Badger. 'But I think ten minutes is long enough to wait without being noticed.'

'My dear Badger!' exclaimed Toad, delighted and relieved. 'A thousand apologies. How very rude of me. My dear old friend! You must come in this minute and tell me what you think. Now you'll speak up for me, won't you? Good, sound business-sense, has our Badger; eh, what? I can't seem to persuade these fellows here that a chap's got to advertise if he's to get on. Now tell them, old boy, eh?'

Badger came in and took a snorter from the whisky decanter being proferred him. He gave a thoughtful rub to his nose with a coat-sleeve, and smoothed back his whiskers.

'Well now,' he said. 'The way I see it is this. You are quite right to air the issues as to whether or not advertising is desirable in itself. And Rat and Mole were quite right to draw attention to some of the near-dishonest claims and to the psychological ploys which are used. But by now you should realize that it's useless trying to convince each other either that advertising is a "good" thing or a "bad" thing. That's a waste of time. If blame has to be attributed it can be placed either on Toad or the gullible public or both: whichever you like. Besides, we've got to look at the practicalities of the situation. You couldn't stop Toad advertising even if you wanted to. And you can't stop people wanting to know about holidays. All you can do – and perhaps all that it's right to do – is to make sure that Toad gives correct and fair information and that people understand the techniques he is using in his advertisements.'

'So the argument stops here,' said Toad, rather firmly.

'Not necessarily,' countered Badger. 'It depends on whether you want to move on to understand more deeply why it is that you hold the different opinions you do. Surely it isn't simply that you see your-selves in the roles of exploiter and exploited? That would be far too naive a distinction. I think the truth may lie deeper. I wonder whether you set the same values on money, possessions, comfort, freedom of choice? I wonder whether you would agree on what were the most important human qualities and motives? If you really wanted to explore your differences of opinion, you might find that there were basically different attitudes and assumptions governing your views of advertising. The only way to understand the argument is to dig for the roots of disagreement.'

'Yes, Badger; how very sensible of you,' Mole nodded.

'Yes. Let's close the subject,' added Rat.

'I agree,' said Toad.

'As a matter of fact, we haven't time to do anything else,' said Badger. 'You know that the weasels are seething with anger over your use of Toad Hall for holidays? On my way here I saw a whole crowd of them in the village, in an ugly mood by the looks of them; and I'm pretty sure that they're getting ready for a surprise attack. If I were you I'd get out of here without a moment's delay. In fact if I hadn't been side-tracked by your argument on Toad's advertisements. . . .'

But at that moment a loud knocking came from the front door.

Further help for the teacher

Suggested teacher's aim

To make children consciously aware of the techniques used in advertising and of their own assumptions in approaching this topic; to make them aware of some of the moral questions raised in certain techniques; to consider the nature of 'propaganda' and 'indoctrination' in general.

Badly handled this topic can easily blur and become flabby, losing all clarity of thought and definition. Similarly over-simplication ('Is advertising wrong?' etc.) seems to children unreal, raising as it does many non-questions. But for the teacher who is prepared to prepare, this is a well documented topic.

General books: R. Harris and A. Seldon, *Advertising in Action*, Hutchison 1962; R. Harris and A. Seldon, *Advertising and the Public*, Hutchinson 1962; J. Tunstall, *The Advertising Man*, Chapman & Hall 1964, which surveys the work of agencies.

Books relating primarily to America: V. Packard, *The Hidden Persuaders*, Longmans 1957, which has become a classic in its field; S. S. Baker, *The Permissible Lie*, Peter Owen 1968.

The poster as an advertising medium: J. Barnicoat, *A Concise History of Posters*, Thames & Hudson 1972; M. Rickards, *The Rise and Fall of the Poster*, David & Charles 1971.

Very useful for reference by teacher and class is *Which* magazine, published by the Consumers Association (14 Buckingham Street, London WC2N 6DS). Then there is obviously the large amount of advertising material which the class can itself collect: posters, magazines, newspapers. The teacher's role is to encourage a critical examination of this, raising questions such as 'Do particular types of product use particular types of appeal? How much does the type of ad, vary from one periodical to another, e.g. the *Sunday Times Colour Supplement* and the *News of the World*? How vague is the wording used?'

Groups could undertake a special study of how a particular type of product – pet food, cosmetics, holidays, books or whatever – is advertised. Handouts, such as one made by the teacher on the role of agencies, can help to give structure. Most important of all is the way in which the teacher deals with the mass of evidence and conclusions of the various groups. He must see that implications in the evidence are drawn out and discussed and that members of the class have done more than amass a scrap book of adverts. Have they understood techniques? Have they understood problems raised by the presentation of some advertisements? Are they as consumers a little more critical and self-aware? As usual in discussion-orientated work the teacher is crucial.

But for the teacher who is prepared to structure his topic carefully this is one of great interest to children. It is worth doing with all groups, but perhaps especially 'ROSLA' children, who are in many ways the least critical consumers of tomorrow, and in fashion, the pop scene, etc., of today. More able children may well use this as an introduction to a more academic study of the nature of propaganda and its recent history, or the nature of indoctrination. A sixth-form General Studies group may well want to work on this aspect. Or again it is a hardy, but useful, perennial in inter-disciplinary work.

CHAPTER FOURTEEN

Murder at SCM Press

'I KNEW,' SAID THE EDITOR'S SECRETARY,' that it was going to be one of them days. First I snagged me tights, then I walked under a ladder and now I get here the Editor's got himself bumped off.'

She was certainly right. The Editor lay, head on the desk, with a dagger in his back, just as she had found him. By now the police had arrived in the personable entity of Chief Inspector Baker, a burly man who was walking round the room looking for clues. He paused by the piano.

'I'm looking for clues,' he said importantly, 'Nobody must move anything.' This remark was rather pointless for the secretary had gone downstairs to nail her files and the Editor couldn't move a thing. Chief Inspector Baker looked round. Somehow it didn't make sense. Nothing appeared to be disturbed. The wine cupboard was untouched and the sherry was still at the chalk mark on the bottle. The points on the model railway were at the right position for 0900. The portrait of the founders, S, C and M was still intact. The manuscript heaps from budding authors lay obviously untouched – as the layer of dust proved – by the side of the Editor. Nothing was different, nothing. And yet . . . gazing idly at the dagger the eagle eye of the policeman noticed that affixed to it was a piece of paper, pinned to the back of the unfortunate Editor. This must surely throw some light on the affair. Prising it carefully from around the dagger (by using his pen-knife attachment for getting stones out of horses' hoofs) Chief Inspector Baker could clearly read the words. It said TRESPASSERS W.[1]

1. Those who have not had the benefit of a classical education should see A. A. Milne, *Winnie-the-Pooh*, Methuen 1926 (paper 1965), chapter 3, for a possible origin of this obscure message.

His thoughts were interrupted by the reappearance of the secretary.

'Here you are,' she said, 'I've made us all a nice cup of coffee.' They sat down to enjoy the premature elevenses. Downstairs they could hear the voice of the housekeeper in heated argument:

'Well, I don't care whether you're from Special Branch or the moon, you ain't walking over my clean floor to get in there and that's final.'

Low voices could be heard in reply, but the housekeeper was not to be talked down.

'And what I say,' she declaimed,' is enough is enough. I don't go breaking my back on 'and and knees to scrub this floor so the likes of you can walk all over it.' A pause.

'I don't care if there's fifty dead in there, you ain't going in till the floor's dry.'

'Oh dear,' thought Chief Inspector Baker, 'it never happens like this in the films.'

By late afternoon the situation was more in hand. The housekeeper was being held 'to help police with their enquiries' at Tottenham Court Road Police Station. This ensured that the police could get in and out of the publishing house without fear of the reprisals. The Editor had been moved, so that the correspondence in his In-tray, into which he had fallen, could be dealt with. A young police constable had a smarting cheek for holding the secretary's hand for rather too long during finger-printing, and the Associate Editor had irrigated her budding jungle in the window box. All was well, except for one thing. They were no further ahead in their investigation than they had been in the morning.

Special Branch Chief Superintendent Claud Smudge, having managed to get in, had taken over the enquiry. He was rather like a Dürer woodcut of a peasant, made the more lifelike by a persistent pursing of the lips and semi sneer on his face. Since the secretary was very busy in the Editor's office, he was holding a conference in the Gents Cloaks to ascertain what to do next.

'It seems,' he sneered, going over the facts, 'that the motive was not robbery. Whoever did this did it out of enmity. Now let's go over the facts. We know that publishers have no friends, they just have authors. It therefore follows that all those who have written books for SCM are suspect. We must trace all these people and check their alibis. Then there's the weapon. That has "Made in Sheffield" engraved on it. We must conduct house-to-house enquiries in Sheffield to see who made it. As to the note, we must submit it to a graphologist for examination.' He leered in the direction of the bath and continued, 'We must find out if anyone suspicious came in this morning.' Glaring at the roller towel he went on, 'These enquiries must move quickly. The Editors of all religious publishing houses are at risk until we have apprehended the skilful criminal behind this. Finally,' he paused, 'MIND YOUR FEET!' The 1700 Inter-City to Glasgow came rushing through the model railway.

The city of York has the sort of summer weather which people in the know call 'muggy'. A sort of oppressive warmth assails the body and lethargy is the result. It was on such a day in early July, almost at the end of the academic year, when man goeth to his long home, that Eustace Blank arrived late for the seminar of which he was a student member, at St John's College. Eustace Blank was not, as the educationalists say, a highly motivated, project-orientated, fully integrated student. He was not troubled by wondering on what Piagetian level of thinking his mind worked. Not for him the careful introspection of the post-Freudian approach to group dynamics. As a matter of fact he preferred fish and chips. Why, then, was he going to a seminar on such a hot afternoon? The answer lay in the lecturer – a sharp-tongued man who caned absent students with sarcasm on their return – and the topic, moral education in schools, which to Eustace implied sex which in turn aroused interest. At least this was the impression Eustace liked to give. Eustace slunk to the back of the class.

'. . . So,' the tutor was saying, 'the main problem with a topic like friendship is to compress a very indistinct topic into some sort of form that children can grasp, without being wishy-washy. They've got to feel that the topic has an aim, that they're making progress by thinking through an orderly body of knowledge and ideas. Otherwise you've just got an aimless waffle on your hands.'

'Easier said than done,' said a girl student at the front.

'I agree,' said the tutor, 'anyone got any ideas?'

'Tell them at the start what the aim is. You couldn't be more explicit.'

'Group question sheets with clearly organized questions to illustrate major points in the discussion?'

'Case studies? The lower ability especially could get their teeth into that.'

'But what would be the aims?' the tutor prodded the group again. Lethargic silence. The afternoon sun shone in, gently sapping their energy. The tutor tried once more.

'Would you say,' he argued, 'the aim would be to make the children more friendly?'

'No,' said a hairy tee-shirted student, 'if you do that you are trying to induce moral attitudes.'

'But you do that when you do anything, like make the class shut up so you can teach,' said a fragile girl who wished that they had shut up on her recent teaching practice.

'Might an aim be to explore the levels on which we experience friendship and the differing demands it makes?'

'Then you could talk about the dangers of manipulating people to make them what we want them to be, instead of letting them be what they are.'

'Could you bring in literature to support the discussion and provide talking points?' The course of the discussion changed.

'How far would you regard the problems of dealing with friendship as typical of the problems posed in moral education?' asked a tall student, hiding behind a bushy beard.

'Fairly typical,' said the tutor, 'partly because it's hard to give it a content, partly because like a lot of ME it can sink into platitudes . . . and children often see through this more quickly than those who teach them.'

'It does seem bodiless,' said another student, 'not the sort of stuff to attract new RE teachers.'

'That depends on the balance in the syllabus between "M" and "R" overall,' said the tutor, 'though some people try to bring a bit of "R" in by talking about, say, David and Jonathan as a biblical example of friendship.'

'You don't rate that?' asked another student.

'It's too much like religion tacked on the end as a mere option and nothing more – and anyway how far is David and Jonathan's friendship anything to do with religion, just because it happens to be in the Bible?'

A Christian Union evangelical student looked critical.

'Well,' said the tutor sensing the disapproval, 'in RE for too long we made the mistake of identifying what is biblical and what is religious. But that opens up a whole new issue. . . .'

Eustace Blank was losing heart. Would the seminar never end? It did at last, though with an injunction by the tutor to them all to produce a specimen lesson as a trial run for the next seminar. And one other thing happened that cheered him. The police came on campus to interview the tutor, who'd written some sort of book for SCM Press to ask him where he'd been on a certain morning. Routine enquiries, they *said*. The tutor had said some very unfriendly things in reply. . . .

Meanwhile in Sheffield investigation reached an impasse. The 'Made in Sheffield' dagger was a Hong Kong imitation.

The Home Office consultant on graphology was Sir Ten (Tennessee from an American mother) Ffacte. His booklined study overlooked a quiet walled garden in the residential part of Wapping. It was there that the case took an unexpected leap forward.

'Now look here,' he said to Chief Superintendent Smudge, 'I've given this paper a lot of my time (he brandished the TRESPASSERS W) and this is my conclusion. The writing is by a man, probably with oriental, perhaps with Hong Kong connexions. You can see that by the way he writes the "S".' Smudge scowled.

'I can also tell you,' Sir Ten continued, 'that he sees himself as an expert on moral education. See how the "T" is crossed with a propriety almost Victorian in moral tone. The "E" is reminiscent of the Schools Council Moral Education Project. Now a man who knew about that would know about clear aims. The Teacher's Handbook to their "Lifeline" series, for example, and what a fine use there of case studies.'

'What about more on this case?' said Smudge, looking darkly at a leather-bound volume.

'Well, I'd take a further guess that he left the second word unfinished to keep us guessing. A real educationalist. Letting his students reach their own conclusions, if they've grasped the aims. Only we haven't grasped them yet.'

'You don't think the "W" means he was interrupted?'

'No, certainly not. It's too rounded off – look at the stylistic flourish at the end.' Smudge looked, and grunted.

'You can't tell us any more?'

'No, not really.' Smudge turned to go. 'Only,' continued Sir Ten, 'that he is an RE teacher trained at St John's College, York.'

'Whaaaaaaaaat?' Smudge was astounded.

'Oh, yes,' continued Sir Ten calmly, 'he must have studied under one of their lecturers, who always insisted on clear aims, lively impact, movement in a lesson and hated fudgy moral education. There's only one man he could have studied under, I think he's called Cotton or Copland or something.'

'I'd better get off to York,' said Smudge.

'Well you won't see Collins or whoever he is,' said Sir Ten, 'he was assassinated last year by a rival called Weston.'

'I can get a list of his students,' said Smudge and with that parting shot he stomped off.

Action was swift. A phone call to York and careful checking with shipping and airlines indeed established that a student of St John's had visited Hong Kong in the summer of 1975. A student who, moreover, had gained an unexpected distinction in moral education. Squad cars rushed Smudge and the Vice Squad to his home address, a flat in the depths of Balham. Sirens still blaring, Smudge leaped out.

'Jacob Snakovski alias Nigel Nihil alias Eustace Blank: this is the police alias the fuzz alias the bluebottles. Open up!' No reply. The door stood ajar. Smudge pushed it open and walked in. The empty room was littered with piles of papers and a small printing press stood in the corner. A light bulb hung from the ceiling, half covered by a serviette in the interests of decency. A half-smoked cigarette, still smoking, lay in the ashtray.

Smudge cast his eye over the room. 'Well,' he exclaimed, 'a nice little nest we've got here.' Feeling that some further comment was called for he tried casting his eyes over the room a second time. 'Phew! The place is littered with moral education, positively littered. There's no doubt about it, this is our man all right. Just look at that Eros dressed up in a mackintosh. And the Ten Commandments over the bed. And the books! Pooh, Alice, Goldilocks! This is stuff for the Vice Squad.'

He went over to the desk. As he saw the slip of paper he took a sudden gasp, and exhaled slowly in a long, low whistle. 'Looks like we got here just in time,' he said as he picked it up, its lettering still wet. It read TRESPASSERS W. 'We'll take all this literature away.' The Vice Squad set to work. Piles of printed leaflets, posters and books were loaded into the cars: left-wing pamphlets on the need to promote unfriendliness;

leaflets on how to use education to divide; tracts on how to run boring discussion lessons; incitements to waffle on moral questions in the hopes of killing off the subject; a whole tome on how to devise timeless lessons devoid of aims and content, with a long chapter on lessons on friendship showing how to conceal the beginning, the end and the aim of the lesson.

'Tricky customer,' muttered Smudge, 'Double agent. Set the place up as a moral education centre, but look at the notepaper. It's headed MESS. This, my lads, is nothing less than the headquarters of the Moral Education Subversion Society. This is the man who's been wrecking ME in schools up and down the country. And to think he was training all the time with this in view. . . .'

'But,' wavered Smudge as he paused to pick his nails, 'why kill the Editor of SCM Press? There's only one place we can find the answer.'

It was now quite late at night. They obtained the pass key for SCM Press and went straight up to the Editor's office (taking care to avoid the night express to Aberdeen). S, C and M gazed down on them coldly from the picture frame. A stillness filled the room, an odour of sanctity and scholarship. The cuckoo-clock chimed eleven. Smudge went straight to the pile of manuscripts by budding authors.

'Of course!' he said. 'This has got to be the answer!' The top script gave it away. The Editor had been going to publish a book on RE and ME aims and methods, called *A Bedside Book for RE Teachers*. This could have undermined all the work of MESS. The motive became perfectly clear.

But his thinking was disturbed by a crash in the Book Room below and it was here that the final scene was to be enacted. They rushed down the stairs to the unlit room and switched the light on. A scene of confusion greeted them. The books, normally neatly arranged on the shelves for sale, were scattered all over the floor. Pamphlets and tracts subverting RE were all over the room, some inserted cunningly into SCM books. Clearly in a desperate last bid to bring down RE and ME throughout the land Eustace had been captured. For as he pursued his evil designs in the darkness of the Book Room he had made one major error. The model railway! He had trodden on the guard's van of the night express to Aberdeen, slipped, fallen and dislodged on to himself 1,000 copies of a hardback text on moral philosophy – a crushing blow which proved his undoing.

'Well,' said the Editor's secretary next morning as she manicured her nails, 'it all adds to life's gay pageant, doesn't it?' The housekeeper nodded in assent as, freshly released from custody, bottom proudly in the air, she scrubbed the steps.[1]

Further help for the teacher

We grasped the nettle of this topic so as not to dodge one of the key problems of all moral education – lack of a clear content. It is this lack of clarity which obviously destroys so much teaching in this area, since it is all too easy for the teacher not to have defined his own boundaries and aims in approaching it. Even with clarity, a diet of too many such topics can give educational indigestion to the pupils unless set into a context of 'traditional' or academic topics, such as some that we have discussed in this book. A useful article on this problem of ME can be found in Chapter 8 of the *Schools Council Working Paper 36, RE in Secondary Schools*, Evans/Methuen Educational 1971.

The best material on this for teacher and pupils is the Schools Council Moral Education *Lifeline* kit, and the accompanying handbook by P. McPhail, published by the Longman Group in 1972. The teacher's greatest qualification in this area is sensitivity. The popular press problem columns may be used, or the Radio 4 programme *If you think you've got problems*, where appropriate questions are posed. Case studies are also vital to this exercise, and those you construct don't sound as corny to the children as some of the commercial ones which they feel don't relate to the real world at all.

This can also lead into a study of the nature of love; poetry (as in Walt Whitman), novels, comics and biblical material might all play a part in such an exploration. Sometimes useful ad hoc discussions of sexual problems may arise; these are not without dangers for the teacher and we have commented elsewhere about the disaster of the 'RE and sex man' (*What they never told you about RE*, pp. 55f.). Suffice to say here that where 'sex' comes into RE it is better that questions should be raised spontaneously by the children with a teacher they

1. Model railway apart, the deceased would have had to confess, had he survived, that Messrs Copley and Easton have caught more than a few of the salient features of life at SCM Press and that any resemblance to characters still living is more than coincidental. Next time they are invited to sherry, if there is any left, it will be with blindfolds (RIP).

know well than that it should occur in a contrived way on a syllabus, which can cause acute embarrassment to pupil and teacher alike. Moreover, it is depressing to note that it is often the teachers who can't stop talking about sex and sex education that are the most unsuited to talk to children about it anyway.

So we repeat: lesson plans must be *extra* clear on the subject of friendship – and they can include plenty of creative work by the group. An aim? We suggest: To encourage children to think more deeply about personal relations and in particular the nature of friendship, by creating for them and encouraging them to create the sort of case studies and discussion situations that widen their own experience and outlook. Don't run the topic for too long; it will easily blur and produce cliché and boredom. Why run it at all? Because relationships matter, and yet so many people enter into them unthinkingly and insensitively.

Should you wish to approach this via literature, we suggest the following books provide useful material:
George Eliot, *Adam Bede* or *Middlemarch* (the character of Dorothea Brooke); Charles Dickens, *The Pickwick Papers* for the Pickwick-Weller relationship, or the fellowship of the club itself. *Great Expectations* can be interpreted as a study in real and false friendship and, of course, *David Copperfield* is a semi-autobiographical novel about a lonely boy's search for friends. Margaret Drabble, *Jerusalem the Golden*: Clara, the heroine, befriends Clelia. For a close, but ultimately sterile, friendship, cf. Birkin and Gerald in D. H. Lawrence, *Women in Love*; John Osborne, *Look Back in Anger*, and the triangular relationship there also provides useful material.

As with biblical texts, much harm can be done by lifting passages out of context – sensitivity is called for yet again.

Classroom Discipline — Some Hints

Inexperienced teachers and students on practice often worry about discipline in the classroom. In one sense they have good cause; anyone who has ever been in a school will know that teachers of many years' experience can produce riots of the highest quality. Nor do those senior colleagues help who nod their heads wisely and say to the novice: 'It's all a question of personality. You've got it or you haven't and that's the end of the matter.'

Of course there is some truth in this – your personality obviously counts and affects the approach you adopt, but you can be helped, at least in avoiding some of the elementary mistakes. Surprisingly little help seems to be given in teacher-training, or by Heads of Department, on this vital issue. It does not pay to listen too much to the wild rumours that circulate about the deterioration in discipline in secondary schools, nor does it pay to accept the way in which some children are labelled as bad, vindictive, disruptive, etc., in staff-room conversation. They may not treat you like this, and until they show signs of doing so you must assume that they won't; your personality and approach may 'click' where others have failed. Respect for those being taught engenders respect for the teacher; classes rapidly see through the nine-to-four teacher, or the teacher who has written them off as thick. Good discipline springs from your enthusiasm to teach them, your enthusiasm to teach them RE, and your command of the subject. If, then, the issue is as simple as that, why do some people end up with problems?

One elementary mistake is to bore the children. The new teacher too often has a tendency to teach down (he has been frightened by the word 'academic') and often does not stretch a class intellectually far enough. Or he over-estimates their power of listening and talks too much, leaving them switched off some way behind him. He may overestimate the capacity of fifteen-year-olds to sustain a discussion without any form of written break in the activity – in general a twenty-minute maximum is the limit. Not to exercise individuals in written skills, as a result of too much discussion, or too many group activities, can also cause boredom. Boredom in the classroom is dangerous, leading as it does to misbehaviour. This can be avoided by careful attention to lesson structure at the planning stage, coupled with adaptability to class reaction as it is delivered.

Coupled with this is the second root cause of lesson failure: lack of impact. This is where the teacher's enthusiasm counts, and his command of the material in question, with a clear sense of his aims in using it. He must know what he is doing and why; the lesson should make this clear to the class in such a way that a hypothetical HMI (there are a lot about!) at the back of the class could almost write out the teacher's aims, lesson plan, etc., even though he had no prior knowledge of the contents of the lesson. Impact is also helped by efficiency and punctuality. The teacher who loses 4C's homework, or turns up late for the lesson (because the last-minute fag in the staffroom delayed him) or even – despite a permissive society – dresses scruffily: this is the teacher whom the children see through very quickly. Shabby teaching produces a shabby response. There will always be one failure who will sit in the staffroom moaning about how badly behaved the children in 'this school' are. Ignore him and his ways. There are no doubt 'bad' individuals – few schools are without them – but the great majority of children behave exactly as we allow and encourage them to behave. They will respond to consistent, fair and firm handling. There is something to be said, with younger children, for a formal beginning (standing) and a formal dismissal to the lesson. Anathema to trendy shabbies, this nevertheless sets the tone. We are sadly lacking in professional attitudes at times; teachers are there to teach! Some confuse this with the desire to be well in with the children. Oddly enough, as seasoned teachers reading this will know, these people are those whom the children like and respect least.

Another cause of lesson failure is bad or unsuitable material. It is mostly Heads of Department who are more able to remedy this, but a teacher who feels he is called upon to teach unsuitable material should certainly make firm representations in the departmental meeting. The sort of thing we are talking about is the sort of syllabus that does AV Bible work with remedials, or the history of the Jews from Abraham to Herod with third years, or the journeys of St Paul, or sex questions with first years, or simply the dreary pilgrimage through the old Bible-based syllabus of the 1930s. Too much of this still, alas, goes on, and children can hardly be blamed for kicking against it.

Another root cause of behavioural difficulties is lack of vigilance on the teacher's part. Sometimes this is a case of going round to answer individual questions and not turning and looking around the rest of the class while talking to the child in question. Sometimes this is the almost deliberate ignoring of a piece of misbehaviour in the hope that it will go away (nerves?); in practice it will usually get worse and eventually spread. When you ask for silence you must have it; never talk over noise. Sometimes the lack of vigilance lies in not chasing defaulters in such matters as homework. It's all too easy, on Friday Period 8, not to hold an inquisition into missing homework, but it is a temptation which must be fought, because two pieces of missing home-work this week become four next, ten the week after, and so on. In all matters of misbehaviour it's better to act at the outset than let it grow. Confucius might have said:

'Wise teacher tell boy off for untied shoe; he never have fight in his lesson.' You take the point. . . . .

But suppose, despite these suggestions, something does go wrong, then how is it best to be tackled? A firm, brief reprimand is usually sufficient if a direct stare has failed. The emphasis must be on brevity; shrill nagging or whining tends to promote hostility. Sarcasm breeds repression; better 'Stop that, Charles,' than, 'Look at Charles again, always the big mouth. . . .' In the second statement you not only make Charles resentful that you've abused your position of authority in order to make personal remarks to humiliate him, you also encourage him to play up to the image of Charles the Mouth in subsequent lessons. Thus 'Now 4C, you're your usual noisy selves today,' is much less preferable than 'How rude you are!', an appeal more to their adult side perhaps combined with 'I don't expect behaviour like this from you', a statement of your professional intention (you *will* teach them!) and a flattering appeal.

Avoid all rhetorical and meaningless questions: 'Am I going to have to wait all day for silence?' 'Are you going to settle down?' Also steer wide of 'I shan't tell you again,' which, if it means anything, means they can now misbehave without further reprimand. If only one person is out of line in a sea of children working silently, don't shout across the whole class, disturbing them and making him into a hero; go up to him, face to face, and talk quietly (which is actually more sinister!) and tell him to get on with his work. Never clap for silence; you merely applaud the noise by clapping, and anyway in the present generation of children some are bound to join in! In general it is not advisable to send children out of lessons for misbehaviour. In the first place this rewards them – they didn't like the lesson and you allowed them to opt out. Equally important they can then distract the class by misbehaving outside the room. Then there's the legal question – if they're found drowned in the washbasins, or hanging from the ceiling by their braces you can be held responsible, at least in law, for failing to exercise 'reasonable supervision'.

Sometimes it pays to detain an individual at the end of the lesson, either to read the riot act, or to appeal to his adult side on a 'man to man' basis. He is then deprived of the support and admiration of the gang. Sometimes a written imposition works, or a lunch-time detention to complete work. This latter can sometimes be more effective than the traditional end of day detention, because it deprives the parties involved of their social life in the lunch hour, after they've eaten the meal itself. You can catch up with your marking! In the case of a written imposition to be done in the pupil's own time give a clear warning first. Otherwise if you just lash out with it, the pupil feels justifiably that this is not fair and you deprive yourself of another stage in the sanction process (reprimand-further reprimand-final warning-imposition of sanction). Most teachers feel, rightly, that to send children to more senior staff is an admission of defeat. This ought not to prevent staff from discussing difficult children (without the children being present) and how to handle them. Discussions of this sort are much rarer than they ought to be, because for some staff there's a loss of prestige in admitting that they have any difficulties at all.

Some schools have a system of being 'on report' for difficult children, whereby teachers have to sign a sheet on their behaviour (i.e. the behaviour of the children in question!) which in due course is scrutinized by a senior member of staff. This can reform some hard cases! We duck the question of corporal punishment here, simply because this is almost never needed or used by the classroom teacher for classroom conduct, and because there are much wider issues involved here, both legal and (for some) moral. Suffice to say that it is extremely inadvisable for the young teacher to employ this; and if he should at any

time strike a child he ought to make a full report, that day, to his Head
and possibly his union.

But this is sounding a rather pessimistic note, coming at the end of
an attempt to provide practical help by saying 'If this fails then. . . . and
if that fails then. . . . and if that fails then. . . .'. In the classroom of the
keen, alert, firm teacher, who is also relaxed and at ease with his class,
problems rarely arise and can easily be met. These are the positive
qualities one should try to emulate added perhaps to a willingness to
take time over and with children, both in school social activities and
in extra sessions for those with genuine learning problems. These can
be as important as lesson contact time, or pupil teacher ratio. A pre-
paredness to engage in promoting high standards of behaviour in
corridor, dining-room, sports-field etc. also helps classroom relations.
The teacher who is only interested in maintaining order in his 35-
minute period may finally be lucky to achieve even that.

So don't worry too much about discipline. Look to the syllabus, the
lesson plan, your own interest and determination to succeed. Try to
keep physically fit – this isn't in case you're attacked, but any experienced teacher knows how much more 'on top' of the job you feel if
you're physically well! Be sure your aims in teaching a topic are clear
to you and the children. You can't teach successfully without discipline,
but if you follow the positive advice you will find that it 'just comes'
and who knows, you might just catch yourself confidently saying 'It's
all a question of personality. You've either got it or you haven't and
that's the end of the matter.' Then you know you're getting old. . . .

LAST WORD

Dawn is worth getting up to see at least once in a lifetime. If you go and stand in the quiet street you can see the hint of a glow start at the skyline and sense the silent expectancy of the new day. Even in cities the very air seems cleansed and the day with its myriad opportunities and possibilities lies ahead. In the cool clean air the past of yesterday recedes. The silence itself demands the song of the birds. If ever you have felt all that, you will know that to put it into words at all reduces it to something almost corny, especially in our antipoetic society. Yesterday with its decisions is history – 4D, the staff meeting and Bedside Books fade away.

If ever the Heavenly City lands it would have to be at dawn, otherwise people would insist that it was a fraud. At dawn they might just accept it. But days soon soil and 4D and the staff meeting come round again. The demythologized West can only try to build the Heavenly City in the real world. It has to be worked for and fought for and lived for. Nothing just comes. And even if you don't feel this archetype or semi-Christian image you know that in the last analysis ideals *do* matter. We see too many cynical or shabby casualties in our staff-rooms, ideals long crushed, to want to lose our sense of what we are about.

Recent history of RE has seen it emerging, dragging itself up from the status of non-subject and it is not yet fully emerged – many headmasters, teachers, parents and politicians really are pig-ignorant of the aims and methods of the New RE and its simple requirement of trained staff, proper timetable allocation and status with (not over) other subjects. For many it still provides scope for attack in order to work out religious or anti-religious bees in their own bonnet.

We believe that those who would demolish ought also to build; anyone can fire negative potshots at a bête noire. Much remains to be done by the writers and readers of this book. What are our ideals in RE? What remains now Christianization is demolished? What ideals are appropriate to the teacher of RE in the new climate of our society?

He may wish to remove misconceptions about religious belief, or impart information on religion, an area of abysmal public ignorance – both short-term goals. He may wish to help each child eventually to reach a conscious stance for living and an awareness and tolerance for alternatives – perhaps the goal of a lifetime. Is this un-Christian? Since Christians have no monopoly of the education system, the question doesn't matter; and in any case it is surely correct to say that this approach is much less un-Christian than attempts to bend and manipulate children towards Christianity, or any belief – Jesus appears to have wanted men to flourish, not to fit into his, or anyone's, rigid pattern; he was not a mind-bender.

We suggest that to walk the water of modern RE teaching is not easy, requiring patience, training and self-knowledge. But it's fun; it works. It has ideals worth fighting for. Get up. Put the Bedside Book down. Turn its dream into reality.

Terence Copley
Donald Easton

INDEX